Strategy in the Public Sector

Wiley Series in Practical Strategy

Series Editor: David Hussey

Published titles

Business Unit Strategy
Segev

Virtual Organizations and Beyond: Discover Imaginary Systems
Hedberg et al.

Strategic Market Planning: A Blueprint for Success
McNamee

Competitor Intelligence: Turning Analysis into Success
Hussey and Per Jenster

Multinational Strategic Alliances
Mockler

Strategy in the Public Sector

A Guide to
Effective Change Management

Paul Joyce

JOHN WILEY & SONS, LTD
Chichester • New York • Weinheim • Brisbane • Singapore • Toronto

Copyright © 2000 by John Wiley & Sons Ltd,
Baffins Lane, Chichester,
West Sussex PO19 1UD, England

National   01243 779777
International   (+ 44) 1243 779777
e-mail (for orders and customer service enquiries):
cs-books@wiley.co.uk
Visit our Home Page on http://www.wiley.co.uk
or http://www.wiley.com

Other Wiley Editorial Offices

John Wiley & Sons, Inc., 605 Third Avenue,
New York, NY 10158-0012, USA

WILEY-VCH Verlag GmbH, Pappelallee 3,
D-69469 Weinheim, Germany

Jacaranda Wiley Ltd, 33 Park Road, Milton,
Queensland 4064, Australia

John Wiley & Sons (Asia) Pte Ltd, 2 Clementi Loop #02-01,
Jin Xing Distripark, Singapore 129809

John Wiley & Sons (Canada) Ltd, 22 Worcester Road,
Rexdale, Ontario M9W 1L1, Canada

Library of Congress Cataloging-in-Publication Data

Joyce, Paul, 1952–
    Strategy in the public sector: a guide to effective change management / Paul Joyce.
        p. cm. – (Wiley series in practical strategy)
    Includes bibliographical references and index.
    ISBN 0-471-89525-3 (hardback: alk. paper)
    1. Public administration.   I. Title.   II. Series.

JF1351.J69 2000
352.3–dc21
                                                                                99-053075

British Library Cataloguing in Publication Data

A catalogue record for this book is available from the British Library

ISBN 0-471-89525-3

Typeset in 11/13pt Times by Vision Typesetting, Manchester.
Printed and bound in Great Britain by Biddles Ltd, Guildford and King's Lynn.
This book is printed on acid-free paper responsibly manufactured from sustainable forestry, in which at least two trees are planted for each one used for paper production.

To Theresa Joyce

Contents

Series Foreword

The aim of this series is to provide managers with books on strategy, strategic management, and strategic change, which are helpful, practical, and provide guidance for the practical application of sound concepts in real situations.

In the mid-1960s when the subject of planning began to emerge, the whole literature could have been listed on one or two sheets of paper. It was easy to decide which books to read, because so few were available. This state of affairs changed rapidly, and the scope of the subject has moved from a focus on formal planning to a broader view which merges with the literature of leadership, change management, strategic analysis and organization. Modern writing sees the organization and its strategies in an integrated way, and there are many, often conflicting, theories about the 'right' way to formulate strategies and practice strategic management.

Management does not take an academic interest in theories, but is concerned about what works best in the situation in which it operates. Hence this series. Each book is conceptually sound, and gives proper acknowledgement to the originators of concepts and ideas, but the emphasis is on using the concept or methods, rather than academic argument.

Business school faculty and students are also concerned with the application of theories and will find much in these books to supplement the more academic texts.

In this series the aim is to give the reader clear guidance on how to make the subject of the book work in his or her own situation, while at the same time taking care to ensure that the books do not over-simplify situations. Check lists and questionnaires are included when they aid the aims of the book, and examples are given. The experience of the author in actually applying the concepts, rather than just knowing about them, is intended to show through the writing.

The series will make complex matters understandable. We hope that it will become a catalyst that helps managers make a difference to the strategic performance of their organizations.

David Hussey
Visiting Professor in Strategic Management
at Nottingham Trent University
and Managing Director of David
Hussey & Associates

Preface

Governments on both sides of the North Atlantic, as well as else-where in the world, have developed public policy in a way that places a great deal of responsibility on managers to bring about radical improvements in the public services. They have given form to this responsibility by adopting strategic planning as a framework within which managers are made accountable to politicians for the performance of public service and the use of public money. For example, in the case of Britain this framework has been an import-ant element in the modernising government agenda. To some extent it followed the example set by the United States of America through the Government Performance and Results Act 1993 that established strategic planning as a universal requirement at the federal level.

It is not yet obvious whether strategic planning and performance management will prove an effective means of bringing about the scale of improvements sought by Governments. If managers carry through the new strategic planning and performance management systems mechanically, it seems safe to predict that they will not work that well. This is because strategic planning and performance man-agement will be developed for a public sector which is evolving away from its bureaucratic traditions. It is a public sector that is getting closer in touch with the public and seeking to harness the powers of partnership and innovation. It is a public sector that aspires to greater openness and learning and is aiming at continuous improve-ment. Managers in top positions within the public sector need to think about how they can apply their experience and expertise to the implementation and use of these new systems. I would expect that they would do so. These top managers operate in a complex and dynamic world where leadership and creativity are essential features of their daily experience.

This book is an attempt to systematise some of the lessons of public sector management experiences in bringing about effective strategic change. It is based on talking to top managers in local government, health services, and education. It represents my attempt to classify and organise the knowledge that practitioners of top management have gained through their own experience. It also attempts to present insights from empirical research on strategic change in the public sector, which is unfortunately still very sparse.

The book has been written to make the lessons of experience and insights from research accessible to experienced and new managers in the public sector. It should also be of interest to students of public sector management who need a book on strategic change written from a management viewpoint. It contains many suggestions about the necessary elements of a comprehensive approach to strategic change. These suggestions can be, in my opinion, extremely valuable to any existing top managers who are interested in deepening and rounding out their thinking on the management of strategic change, as well as to any individuals who have recently moved into positions of responsibility within management in the public sector. In particular, this book contains suggestions about how to prepare for strategic change and how to consolidate it. It contains very specific suggestions for managing strategic change with the public and through partnership initiatives. I am arguing in this book that there is much missing from the view of strategy that equates it with only drawing up mission statements and strategic goals and then implementing operational changes.

Paul Joyce
London

1
A Model of Effectiveness

STRATEGIC CHANGE IN THE PUBLIC SECTOR

It is often assumed that many managers in the public sector are relative newcomers to the conscious use of strategic management. The rationale for using strategic management seems obvious enough. Through strategic management top managers create the conditions for good organisational performance and for success in the future. But strategic management is a challenging process for top managers. This is not because of the basic theoretical ideas of strategic management. They are not intellectually difficult or arcane ideas. It is the execution that is challenging.

There are two major constraints on top managers. First, they have limited knowledge and this makes knowing what to do problematic. Second, they have a limited ability to impose their decisions and intentions on other people in the organisation and this makes the implementation of strategy problematic. These limitations of knowledge and control exist for managers in all sorts of organisations and are certainly not unique to the public sector. However, in at least some public sector organisations, they are not equally problematic. Knowing what is to be done seems to be less of a problem than implementation. Most large public sector organisations seem to manage the tasks of writing mission statements and identifying who their clients and service users are. These, and other, analytical activities in strategic management are relatively easy to do at a satisfactory level. Implementation activities are more challenging. Managers struggle with the realignment of budgets, processes, and information; they struggle with changing an organisation's culture; and they struggle with developing employee commitment and skills.

There is a long-standing interest in the public sector's organisational capacity to change (Crozier 1964; Osborne & Gaebler 1992; Pettigrew et al. 1992). Politicians are usually elected with a mandate for ambitious developments that require the public sector to change. Pettigrew and his colleagues (1992, p. 6) suggested that ' . . . a fundamental problem in the 1970s was the development within the NHS [National Health Service] of service policies for massive change, without building up the organizational capacity to translate this ambitious change agenda into practice'. The difficulties of making changes are put down to all kinds of things. It is sometimes suggested that, unlike their private sector counterpart, public sector organisations have an extraordinarily rich set of powerful and diverse stakeholders. It may be said that the reliance on elected politicians to provide resources for investment is a problem. Sometimes the difficulties of making changes are blamed on the professionals that are an important force in many parts of the public services. In the past, public sector trade unionism was blamed. And at all times bureaucracy has been seen as a major impediment to change.

The difficulties of implementing change in the public sector may seem to be contradicted by the scale of changes that occurred in the public sector during the 1980s and 1990s. However, it could be argued that the rigidity of the public sector and its low capacity to change meant that change was more violent when it finally came.

This book looks at how strategic change in the public sector organisation can be handled better as a management process. The ideas presented in this book are to be found in practice in a variety of public sector organisations. In many cases, however, the ideas are taken for granted and overlooked. Or they are applied in a fragmented way. Effective strategic change requires that the various elements of good strategic management practice be done properly and combined to form a more comprehensive process of strategic change. For example, there is widespread recognition of the need to make change happen, but there is less appreciation of the need for action to ensure that changes are stabilised and target performance achieved.

In some cases, top managers in the public sector have had to learn the hard way that weak or non-existent links in the chain of strategic change will undermine hard work and sincere efforts to make improvements. A couple of years ago a health service chief executive strongly endorsed the use of performance management systems (PMS). He had learnt its importance from experience. His hospital had a very ambitious strategic plan and he was intent on making root and branch changes throughout the organisation. But the hospital was finding it difficult to maintain changes made at the operational level. Securing innovation seemed a very hit and miss affair. Then the top managers began to pay attention to the performance management system:

> The thing that brought it home to me, was we did a lot of very good work around our stock management and supply system. It looked like something we could fix. New processes were put in place. And it was all done very effectively. And it more or less disappeared within 6 months. Why? The people who actually had to operate it didn't see it as being in their interests to do so. And were not aligned to doing it. And since there was no performance management system that was in place really to check how well they were doing it against baseline performance indicators. No incentive. (Unpublished interview with author, 1997.)

This is just one example of the need for a complete strategic change process. If critical steps are missing or skimped the overall result can be disappointing. So, there is a need for an awareness of all the elements that go into strategic change and how the various elements need to be linked together and managed as a process.

Before we look at a model of the strategic change process, we take a closer look at the special nature of strategic management in the public sector.

PUBLIC SECTOR STRATEGIC MANAGEMENT

The formal system of strategic management in the public sector has emerged only recently and is often based on strategic planning principles. Bushnell & Halus (1992, p. 357) define strategic planning as 'a process that an organization can use to visualize its future and develop the necessary strategies and operations to achieve that vision'. They distinguish it from operational planning and long-range planning (p. 357):

> Unlike operational planning—which stresses how to get things done—and long-range planning—which primarily focuses on translating goals and objectives into current budgets and work programs—strategic planning is also concerned with identifying barriers and issues that need to be overcome if the agreed-upon goals are to be met. . . . Assessing the external and internal

environments that affect an agency receives more emphasis in strategic planning than in long-range planning and, therefore, strategic plans are more likely than long-range plans to incorporate changes in direction and to include a broader range of alternatives.

According to Wilkinson & Monkhouse (1994, p. 16), 'Strategic planning is a means to an end, a method used to position an organization, through prioritizing its use of resources according to identified goals, in an effort to guide its direction and development over a period of time.' These definitions more or less correspond to the intentions behind much of the development of strategic management that took place in the United States, Britain, and elsewhere in the 1990s. In these countries there has been an attempt to apply a model of strategic planning that often features mission statements, strategic goals, and evaluation focused on the measurement of performance gaps. It is designed primarily to enable managers to be held accountable for the performance of their organisation by politicians.

The desire by politicians to make managers accountable for performance has become stronger in recent years. Flynn & Strehl (1996, p. 12), commenting on public sector management in Europe, reported: 'In all the states we examined there have been attempts to redirect managerial effort from conformance to performance.' In the past politicians expected managers to conform to the legal rules and norms. Changes in management behaviour were expected only as a result of changes in the law. In recent years throughout Europe new arrangements have been introduced. These are designed to produce an agreed mission or purpose for the public sector organisation, set up means for measuring performance against targets, and hold managers accountable. Flynn & Strehl's summary of developments in European countries along these lines shows just how widespread these new arrangements are (see box).

The United States has developed a similar strategic management system for federal agencies. This is based on mission statements, strategic goals, annual performance goals, and performance targets. The performance goals are derived from the strategic goals that in turn are related to the mission statement.

While the European countries and the USA have strategic management systems in the public sector that make managers accountable for performance to politicians, they theoretically allow managers more freedom to manage in order to use resources more effectively.

Strategic Management in Europe

The Netherlands government and parliament agreed an approach in 1992, called 'towards more result oriented management', which set out the ways in which the expected results of activities could be formulated into a type of internal contract, similar to a real contract with an external supplier of services. Austria now has a formal system in which political goals are made explicit and then translated into tasks, objectives and projects for officials. In Sweden, the agency objectives and targets are agreed as the planning and budgeting process between agencies and ministries. At Land and city level in Germany, there have been developments of a 'new steering model', which involves, among other things, agreement on outputs and performance. Switzerland has a new 'controlling' system which sets goals, makes priorities explicit, allocates resources and sets up evaluation criteria for performance. In the United Kingdom, departments agree goals and targets with agencies and set the resource and management framework to achieve the targets.
Source: Flynn & Strehl (1996, p. 12).

The formal system of strategic management is not the whole story. The processes by which strategic management actually brings about results and change have also to be considered. Heymann (1987) produced one of the best and most detailed accounts of strategic management in the US public sector. His core proposition is that 'the central challenge of strategy is to make desirable goals, external support, and organisational capacity fit together' (p. 15). This suggests that at the core of strategic management is the co-alignment of these three elements: goals, external support, and organisational capacity. It is worth clarifying what Heymann has in mind for each of these three critical components.

The desirable goals may be contained in a strategic vision of what new activities the organisation should undertake in the future and what new benefits will be produced for the public. In Heymann's analysis of the United States' experience the democratic process influences these goals. The managers are democratically accountable to politicians and thus, in the end, concerned with delivering political objectives. He offers a quite subtle interpretation of the relationship between the democratically elected politicians and the managers. As a first approximation the relationship may be described as a partnership. But, and this is essential to the democratic nature of the relationship, Heymann characterises managers as 'no more' than partners of elected politicians. Moreover, the managers are responsible, along with the politicians, for ensuring that the legitimacy of elected politicians is combined with the vision of the managers.

By external support Heymann appears to mean the support of any person or body that is not subject to managerial control. So, it includes political bodies that have oversight of the organisation and approve funding of its activities. But it also means sections of the public, organised constituencies, and private businesses. These are stakeholders that have needs and might benefit from the new activities or who must accept and co-operate with the activities of the public sector organisation. The top managers may think of the need to obtain external support as being met by a process of forming alliances.

Organisational capacity refers to the fact that organisational members must be able and willing to carry out strategic goals. This may direct top management attention to the skills and capabilities of managers and employees but also to organisational values.

Planning is needed to bring about new activities, external support, and organisational capacities to achieve the desired goals (see Figure 1.1). Heymann uses strategy to mean the goals contained in the vision plus a plan. The most complete of Heymann's statements of strategy is presented in the box.

Heymann identifies many issues for effective strategy in the public sector. For example, he points out that government departments and bureaux cannot be entirely ordered from above and that the 'need for coordination must often be addressed by horizontal arrangements' (Heymann 1987, p. 92). He advises that each agency that shares power and responsibility may seek to define sharp boundaries or act in rivalry. But they may also form alliances to develop interconnecting strategies with other organisations sharing responsibilities.

Heymann's model of strategy is based on his analysis of a number of cases. Some aspects of it seem to be corroborated by a detailed investigation of strategic change in the Ohio Department of Mental· Health during the period 1983–1990. This was regarded as a highly successful experience of strategic change. The researchers,

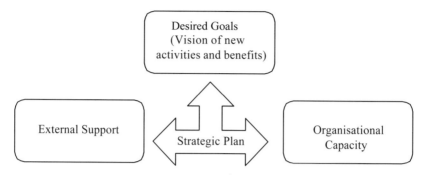

Figure 1.1 Heyman's public sector strategy model

Strategy in the public sector

A strategy goes beyond recognition of a desirable goal that is feasible in terms of internal capacity and external support. A manager also needs to see the broad outlines of a plan for obtaining the needed capacity and support and understand the sequence of major steps leading toward carrying out his objectives. If the goal is not within the present capacity of the organisation, there must be an acceptable means to develop that capacity. If the needed outside support is not there, there must be a realistic way to bring it into being. Finally, the goal and plan—that is, the strategy—must be specific enough to provide guidance on a number of matters, notably, the major priorities in activities to be undertaken by the organisation and the most important organisational steps required to develop the capacities needed to carry these out. For lesser, more isolated decisions, the strategy should also provide an ability to assess their importance in relation to the overall plan and goals. A set of notions that serves these purposes would be a well-developed strategy for the organisation. Source: Heymann (1987, pp. 19–20).

Frost-Kumpf and others, found three important components of strategic action. The first, corresponding to Heymann's idea of a strategic vision, was leadership action to provide an intellectual foresight about the future of the organisation. The researchers described this as symbolic action by the leaders. Secondly, there was action to develop capabilities for management, participation, and planning. This might be seen as corresponding to Heymann's idea of the development of organisational capacity. At a more detailed level, the researchers identified action that they described as building internal capacity, developing technical expertise, and utilising training. The Ohio Department of Health involved consumers along with other constituency groups outside (and inside) the organisation. Perhaps this helped to build external support. Thirdly, there was action to form co-operative ventures with other government agencies. This might be seen as relevant to Heymann's point about government departments and bureaux forming alliances. There is not an immediate and perfect fit between these two models, but there is clearly some 'family resemblance'.

For those interested in looking for similarities and differences with private sector theories of strategic management it may be pointed out that this work of Heymann broadly echoes concerns of resource-based strategy models. For example, in Hamel & Prahalad (1994)'s version of resource-based strategy, attention is paid to the organisation's core competences (i.e. internal capacity), and to the advantages and opportunities of alliances. Perhaps this suggests that at a very general level there is some continuity between the public and private sectors in terms of strategy and strategic change, even if the relationship of the managers to the democratic process is significantly different.

STRATEGIC CHANGE: A LEADERSHIP PERSPECTIVE

Looking at published work on strategic management in the public sector it is obvious that the perspective is usually either academic (in the sense of being designed for students taking courses) or advisory (aimed at novice practitioners). In the former case the perspective tends to be one of writing about the analytical tools and steps of the strategic management process. In the latter case it may offer detailed help on the analytical thinking and writing of strategic plans. Both tend to be weak on the leadership aspects of strategic management for public sector executives.

At the present time public sector leaders are often concerned with questions of the proper and effective exercise of power and persuasion in complex organisations suffering from a crisis of confidence and a hankering after past certainties. Managerial leadership, which is desperately needed in modern public sector organisations, finds itself placed under suspicion by the professionals and administrators of the old public sector. It is also distrusted by that section of politicians that remains wedded to older post-war notions of the public sector. Of course, managerial leadership challenges the rights of professionals to have a monopoly in defining public need, and seeks to innovate in a way, which can be undermining of political authority in the public sector. So, in these ways, professionals and some politicians have a basis for their suspicion of managers talking the modern language of strategic management.

If strategic management is divorced from its managerial leadership aspect in the public sector—if it is seen reductively as a set of analytical techniques for planning and implementing change—it is an impoverished model of strategic management. When strategic management is used effectively in the public sector it does so by confronting the need to use power and influence throughout the organisation. This inevitably means that questions of competing interests are considered not only from the point of view of the academic interested in conflict management, but also from the practical point of view of 'making things happen' and ensuring that strategic changes are seen through to completion.

The following sections outline the major processes of strategic change in the public sector. These were identified using a small number of specially conducted interviews in the health services and local government. These interviews were supplemented by observations made in the course of several research and consultancy projects in the public sector.

There are four key processes in public sector strategic change (Figure 1.2):

1. Preparing.
2. Leading.
3. Changing.
4. Partnering.

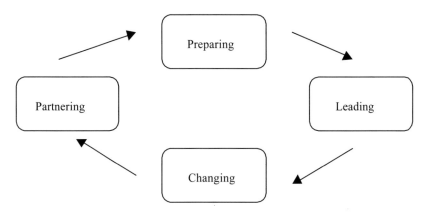

Figure 1.2   Strategic change processes

There are a number of leadership activities associated with each of these strategic change processes.

Preparing

Preparing for strategic change involves top management making sure that the organisation is basically fit to embark on strategic change processes. Successful public sector executives appear to be very interested in assessing the basic functioning or health of the organisations they lead. They weigh up the boards and executive bodies that they work with directly. They do not assume that their boards and their executives are really mentally ready to carry out their responsibilities for providing strategic direction to the rest of the organisation. Public sector executives worry about the functioning of the management systems that are essential to operational efficiency—planning, budgeting, and performance measurement systems. For example, they may find that the organisation is in an unhealthy state because its financial systems are poor and problems of finance constantly divert the organisation from concentrating on defining its mission and delivering it. Senior executives may be concerned to assess how well the managerial infrastructure is working in basic terms. They will look at questions such as: how are managers communicating with each other; is there sufficient co-operation and partnership working within the organisation; are managers clear about who is responsible for what; are the managers confident and optimistic about tackling the challenges that will have to be faced? Effective chief executives in the public sector are quick to diagnose shortcomings in top-level boards and executive bodies, management systems, and the quality of co-operation and purposefulness in the tiers of management. They begin to work immediately on any problems they discover and continue to work on them even when they are working to implement strategic plans.

The senior executives pay attention to the concerns and demands of the politicians that have oversight of their organisation. This principle of effective strategic management is special to the public sector. However, effective public sector executives pay attention to politicians, and their intermediaries, in much the same way that private sector executives pay attention to the market and customers. In some public sector bodies the politicians are quite close to the management of the organisation and may indeed be carrying out a managerial function (e.g. in local government). In other cases public sector organisations may feel that the politicians are more remote. If politicians are making it clear that they are expecting certain results or outcomes from a public sector organisation then it is a foolhardy chief executive who fails to ensure that strategies are put in place which will fairly rapidly produce the desired results.

Preparatory work may be also needed before organisations are prepared to consent to strategic leadership. Leadership is something to be won. It is something managers and employees have in their power to give to a chief executive. For managers and employees make leaders by choosing to follow. This is an issue of trust as much as it is an issue of respect. And trust has to be earned. Leadership is secured in the public sector by senior executive teams showing that they are capable of solving issues. This means that issue management is an important way in which managers become leaders.

Leading

Leadership is about vision and foresight. In the public sector successful chief executives facilitate the development of a long-term vision for their organisation. They may not have the right to be the sole arbiter of the vision. There are always politicians who have a greater right to formulate a vision, but public sector organisations vary in their relationship to politicians. Some have a very close relationship with politicians. The politicians may take a day-to-day interest in how they operate. They are able to work with politicians to define the strategic vision that should guide the direction of the organisation over the long term. Others are more distant from politicians and have to incorporate political messages that have been much mediated by other voices. Either way, public sector chief executives never forget that it is their responsibility to act as an agent of political mandates, and that they usurp this political 'steer' at their peril.

Many public sector organisations have powerful employee interests. Professionals are found in local government, the health services, education, and so on. These groups expect to be listened to and have their views taken into account. Trade union membership levels can be quite high in public sector organisations simply as a reflection of the employment concentrations found in the public sector. Unions exist in part to ensure that ordinary employees are informed and consulted about major organisational changes. Pragmatic senior executives in the public sector are used to involving and consulting their workforce. They use working groups, working parties, diagonal slice groups, and workshops to involve large numbers of managers and ordinary employees in strategy formulation. However, effective executives also know that they must make up their own mind and if need be stick to their guns despite being in a minority. They have a responsibility for effective strategic action that sometimes requires ignoring a consensus or even collegial relations with other executives.

Chief executives and their management teams worry like never before about how they are going to foster leadership at all levels of the organisation. They may think about this in quite mechanical terms. They may plan management development programmes to consolidate management positions throughout the organisation. They may prescribe communication programmes to ensure that these managers are aware of, and committed to, the vision and grand strategy that the chief executive and top management team have launched. They may think about it more organically, and see the pressures and strains of strategic change as providing tests of individuals. Some of the individuals will prove themselves to be managerial material, and others who lack the ability and commitment will leave the organisation because they do lack the ability and commitment.

Changing

Changing the organisation means in part engaging managers and employees with the strategy that is emerging or has emerged. Simply publishing a strategic plan will not do it. It takes unremitting work, and relentless effort, to make strategies real. People are only engaged by a strategy if the managers work very hard at engaging them. Only the most exceptional managers and employees will spontaneously rally around a strategic vision. Indifference, not excitement, is the natural first reaction of most managers and employees to hearing about the organisation's strategic intent and its plans for realising it.

Making changes means focusing and aligning budgets and activities as required by the strategy. Successful executives in public sector organisations know that focusing and aligning the organisation do not happen of their own accord. The strategy has got to be used to focus and align the organisation. Resources and activities have to follow strategy.

Paradoxically, making changes requires efforts to stabilise the changes. An organisational capacity for strategy undoubtedly involves the ability of an organisation to incorporate or stabilise strategic changes. Very often organisations can bid for their members' short-term interest in an issue, but it takes an effective organisation to make changes permanent and not just a temporary appeasement. Successful chief executives are seeing the role of performance management systems at all levels—from organisation-wide to the individual level—as part of the answer. If something is important then it ought to be addressed within performance management systems, and deviations from desired standards of performance addressed through improvement plans. Incentives are also needed.

Partnering

Under contemporary conditions strategic change is not complete when it consists only of activities associated with preparing, leading, and making strategic changes. Under prevailing conditions, chief executives are learning that they and their organisations can only achieve strategic goals and performance levels expected of them if they work with the public and with other organisations. This is at heart a matter of knowing what needs public sector organisations should be addressing and putting together resources from both inside and outside the organisation to meet these needs more satisfactorily. The chief executives have to be able to get their organisations to open up, communicate better with the public, and negotiate with partners to create effective alliances for public interests.

The shift to working with the public and partner organisations can both be described as partnering processes. The public becomes a partner rather than a mere client or passive beneficiary. Other organisations become partners as public sector bodies realise the limitations of an attitude of self-sufficiency that has defined the public sector for over 40 years.

Finally, as partnering proceeds and develops we can see the gradual opening up of public sector organisations. At first this may be concentrated on activities which are required by politicians demanding results-oriented government. Public sector organisations, for example, become less secretive and report openly their performance results in areas identified as critical by politicians. This shift to accountability is supplemented by a greater spirit of responsiveness as public sector organisations become more prepared to adapt to meet public needs, and eventually the organisations move towards the learning organisation format as they strive to learn how they can more effectively serve the public. There is in these evolutions a progressive trend to opening up all aspects of the public sector organisation.

The processes of strategic change outlined above broadly map on to Heymann's model of public sector strategy. The processes of leading are obviously important for establishing effective strategic goals. The processes of changing are important for organisational capacity. The partnering processes will, of course, be critical for getting external support. This link between Heymann's model and strategic change processes is suggested in Figure 1.3.

GUIDE TO THE REST OF THE BOOK

In the preceding section we have outlined the four key activities of strategic change in modern public sector organisations. The rest of this book explores the details of this agenda for strategic leadership.

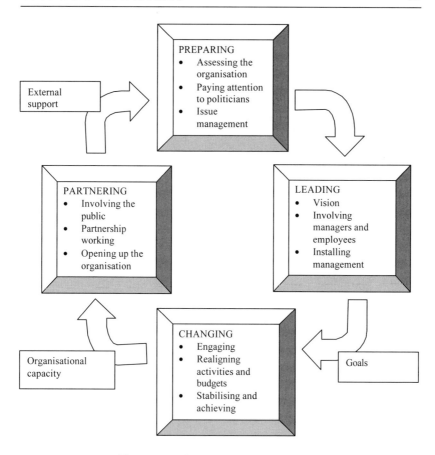

Figure 1.3 Strategic change elements

In Chapter 2 we look at how senior executives assess their organisations. Chapter 3 focuses on the relationship between top managers and politicians, and how the former can be responsive to the requirements of the latter. In Chapter 4 we look at the ways in which top managers can build credibility for their position by addressing and managing issues. Chapter 5 explores how top managers develop long-term visions and points of view about the future of their organisations. Chapter 6 concentrates on activities that are intended to involve others inside the organisation in thinking about the future. Chapter 7 considers the ways in which management is installed in a public sector organisation; this is important for deepening leadership at all levels, which is crucial if strategy is to be effectively carried through. Chapter 8 is concerned with engaging members of the organisation with the long-term strategic intent. Chapter 9 shows the way in which changes are made by getting focus and alignment on the basis of strategy. Chapter 10 sets out the activities needed for stabilising changes and achieving targets, and covers developing performance measuring systems and providing incentives. Chapter 11 looks at the process of involving and consulting the public. Chapter 12 looks at partnership working. Chapter 13 explores the critical process of 'opening up' that is seen as the hallmark of modern strategic change in the public sector. Finally, in Chapter 14, some overall conclusions about the nature of strategic change in the public sector are set out and linked to the modernisation agenda which is currently reshaping the future of this sector.

2
Assessing the Organisation

A new or an existing chief executive must get an organisation
ready for accepting a new strategic direction and for implementing strategic changes. A key aspect of getting the organisation
ready is assessing its current functioning and instigating actions
and alterations that bring about readiness for strategic developments. The new chief executive asks him- or herself: what kind of
shape is this organisation in? Is it ready to embark on a new
strategic direction?

The assessment largely consists of making judgements about the
competence of the organisation in key areas. These judgements
may be based on listening to the views of people throughout the
organisation and analysis of written information. The judgements
should be based on looking at the outcomes achieved by the organisation, and the quality of the services or products produced. In
the future it may be increasingly based on a comparison of actual
results and performance targets and quality standards in performance plans. In the past this has been difficult because of the gaps in
management information systems.

Assessment of the organisation and the remedial action to bring
it up to scratch are ongoing activities. They are not a one-off
exercise timed to precede strategic analysis. However, chief executives in public sector organisations in complex and dynamic environments may feel that they do not have much time in which to
make some initial judgements. They may even allow themselves

only two or three weeks to form some initial understanding of the key issues of organisational health. This is in part because they feel the pressure of external events or problems, but it is also because they are aware that their own managers and employees are expecting them to act. Consequently, a swift assessment may be used by the new chief executive to decide on how they will conduct themselves initially, and what early issues to tackle. The initial assessment may produce a set of key issues and a plan for addressing these issues.

These issues are not strategic issues. The plan for addressing them is not a strategic plan. It may be useful to call them 'organisational issues' and 'organisational development plans' to distinguish them from strategic issues and strategic plans that are longer term. The difference between them is underlined by the fact that the assessment may reveal few organisational issues and little need for an organisational development plan. The organisation may be functioning very well. And yet there may be a major strategic issue. There may be a need for strategic change in order to address a future threat to which the organisation is vulnerable. So, a chief executive with a healthily functioning organisation, which is running smoothly, may still need to develop strategic foresight, set a strategic direction, and bring about strategic changes. On the other hand, a poorly functioning organisation may be in such bad shape that attempts to introduce strategic management processes would get nowhere. Thus, we are making the point that individual organisations in the public sector may need organisational development plans if they are to stand a reasonable chance of successful strategic management.

Pettigrew et al. (1992) studied strategic service changes in the UK National Health Service in the late 1980s. One of their cases was the Bloomsbury District Health Authority. In the autumn of 1985 the authority had a large financial gap between resources and commitments. It was reported that the district general manager 'saw the need to regain financial control within the District as a prelude to strategic control' (Pettigrew et al. 1992, p. 93). This illustrates the precedence that may be given to organisational issues before top managers attempt to carry out strategic changes.

In this chapter we will look at what is assessed for the purpose of producing an organisational development plan and how these plans may be implemented.

POLITICAL HEALTH

In the public sector the assessment of the organisation's functioning may need to look at how well managers are working with politicians. This is particularly the case in local government where elected politicians directly exercise leadership of the organisation. The assessment may recognise that the nature of the politicians as a body is the critical influence on the quality of the relationship between politicians and managers. The managers tend to prefer that politicians be organised as a coherent force with a clear agenda, cohesive in how they operate, and dynamic. While a split and quarrelsome group of politicians may create more space for autonomous management action, an effective political body can create an effective context for high levels of management performance and achievement. Perhaps this is because such a political structure means that political processes work more rationally and predictably, whereas splits and divisions create instabilities and upsets in decision making as a result of power plays and manœuvres to achieve temporary and short-term political advantage. Furthermore, the existence of power plays and manœuvring among the politicians causes much wasted management time. Managers spend a lot of time among themselves discussing management–politicians relationships, speculating on what politicians want, and trying to work out how to work with politicians who are preoccupied with party political matters and not interested in the functioning of the organisation. In contrast, a coherent and cohesive political leadership helps managers to stay focused on getting the work of the organisation done.

Managers do at times express their preference for working in this more ordered type of political setting.

Bloomsbury District Health Authority (referred to above) in the early and mid 1980s illustrated a situation in which a split among the members of the health authority created particular problems for management because professionals formed a powerful alliance with members who opposed retrenchment (see box).

Generalising from the Bloomsbury District Health Authority predicament, we may suggest that managers should be striving to achieve a partnership with politicians that results in a fusion of the legitimacy of the politicians and the strategic goals of the managers (Heymann 1987). There should also be effective relationships between managers and professionals. In the absence of these kinds of

Bloomsbury District Health Authority (DHA)—Early and mid 1980s

In the early 1980s this health authority had a reputation for left-wing politics but was perceived by the regional level of the National Health Service as a conservative organisation that approached change cautiously and incrementally. Pettigrew and his colleagues report that the managers were not exercising strategic control. The regional view of the district was critical. There was, among other problems, 'an alliance between left members [of the DHA] and professionals to put the lid on retrenchment; an inability or even a secret unwillingness of managers to control strategy; and a lack of performance in achieving objectives' (Pettigrew et al. 1992, p. 88).

The District Management Board was alleged by one of its members to have a style of 'endless introspection'; he also claimed that it did not take decisions and 'endlessly agonises about how to get issues through the Health Authority' (p. 88).

Faced with pressures to rationalise services, the district experienced 'severe difficulty' 'in building a consensus around a core strategy' (p. 90). A strategy was pursued but with apparently little success. Pettigrew and his colleagues claimed that the district was finding it difficult to cope with even a modest level of retrenchment: the efficiency savings were failing; 'reserves were being used up; infrastructure was deteriorating further; and the District was moving into escalating overspends' (p. 92). Significantly, it is suggested that, 'As early as late 1983, it was becoming clear to the joint Unit Management Team that the use of medically dominated, single speciality working parties to progress rationalisation was flawed and usually resulted in 'bidding up'; that it was difficult to make substantial savings without coming down on workload; and that the parameters of budgetary review needed to be widened' (p. 92).

relationships it can be difficult for managers to develop strategies that enjoy support internally and externally and that are likely to be effectively implemented.

The assessment of working relations with politicians may look very specifically at the nature of the communications between them and managers. The ideal may be seen as a high volume of communication. The managers may see their part in this high volume as consisting of the provision of advice and recommendations. Managers look for articulate, intelligent, and well-informed politicians. The antithesis is where the level of interaction is high but the politicians are quick to offload responsibilities for mistakes, or are abusive.

REPUTATIONAL HEALTH

A second area for assessment is the health of the public sector organisation's reputation. The chief executive will assess if there is a need to promote the reputation of the organisation. This means making use of PR activities designed to get the right kind of coverage of the organisation in the media. For example, universities want their professors on television and radio and quoted in the newspapers. The amount of coverage matters. Public sector organisations want to be in the public spotlight. The more coverage by the media, the more they must be a leading edge organisation. The assumption is that the best public sector organisations are high profile. In these days of marketing and branding, public recognition is important to leading private sector firms. The importance placed by public sector organisations on good public relations may also be aimed at developing more public recognition. However, the benefits of good PR work quite differently. Public sector organisations may want to achieve a high profile because they perceive that as important in the competition for budget allocations by government. The public sector organisation may be more defensive in its motivation and want a higher profile to reassure the public that it is getting good value for money. Perhaps a high profile is important to individual politicians or managers who see their career being helped by positive publicity. Media coverage, providing it is positive, also helps with the internal morale of the people who work for the organisation.

The top managers see the use of PR activities as a way of positioning the organisation in the wider set of public sector organisations. For example, as governments bring forward their proposals for public sector modernisation, chief executives will be making decisions about how to position their organisation in relation to them. Some will want to take up a position in the vanguard of change. Others will hang back and let other organisations be the first-movers taking the risky experimental moves required by the modernisation agenda. Yet others may take up positions of resistance to changes. Such postures are signalled heavily in the media, and press relations or communications departments will be active in positioning the organisation. Positioning the organisation is only in part a matter of changing strategies and operational activities.

Public sector organisations work hard these days to establish a positive reputation. This seems to be increasingly based on being seen as an innovator. But such is the rate of change that an established reputation as a leader is soon lost as other public sector organisations leapfrog ahead. So, even leading edge, high-profile public sector organisations cannot afford to rest on their laurels, but need to constantly establish new positions in the dynamic kind of world of public sector organisations.

Senior public sector managers read the specialist press for their area of activity (e.g. health, local government, and education). They read what their rivals are telling the press. They compare their activities with those reported. They make their own assessments about how innovative they are by comparison, sometimes noting their own failures to tell the media what they are achieving. There is an awareness that reputations are a function of both actual achievement and successful PR activities to tell others about what has been done.

Public sector organisations do not want bad press and bad publicity. Heymann (1987) suggests that managers of government agencies must pay attention to their 'vulnerabilities'. All public sector organisations have them. 'Almost every program that enjoys the attention of a sizeable public and of the media has, at any given time, its own particular vulnerability to popular attack as well as its own special claims to public support' (Heymann 1987, p. 46). Universities that specialise in wider access may be vulnerable to attacks from the media that they are lowering educational standards in order to succeed. Mental health services provide support to people with challenging behaviour and may be vulnerable to charges of allowing dangerous people to return to the community. Local authorities are valued as a democratic way of organising public services but may be criticised for wasting public money on political causes. Managers may feel it is important to assess whether their current activities are exposing them needlessly to media attacks on these points of vulnerability.

CULTURAL HEALTH

While many managers emphasise in discussion the importance of culture, especially when discussing the prospects for making strategic changes, the cultural issues that have been of most concern centre on just a few matters. These have been accountability, pride, pessimism about change, and complacency.

Many chief executives over recent years have seen the instilling of a culture of accountability as crucial. The implication is that managers and employees avoiding accountability have sometimes undermined public sector organisations. The conditions that create this situation are not clear. Perhaps people avoid accountability because it is easier. Perhaps it is because there is a punitive approach to failure that breeds mistrust and avoidance of responsibility.

Chief executives may also look for a culture in which employees are proud of their organisation, and proud of the work they do. This is linked to organisational achievement. If the organisation is getting good results, and is building a good reputation, then employees should feel proud to be part of it. If there is a culture of disaffection, with employees feeling separated from the organisation and not proud to be working there, the chief executive knows that it is going to be hard to make strategic changes with the support and commitment of employees.

Another cultural dimension concerns the attitude to change. Do managers and employees believe that they work in an organisation that can make changes? If the organisation is suffering from a pessimistic culture, then change is hard to introduce. The constraints on change (such as those resulting from budgetary pressures) may be blamed for this pessimism, but the chief executive who diagnoses a pessimistic culture knows that strategic innovation is going to be hard to engineer. This pessimistic culture finds expression in the claim that the day-to-day pressures of operational activities, the demands of current clients and service users, mean that there is no time to change existing ways of doing things. The organisation must concentrate on what it is doing now.

A culture of complacency is especially shown up by poor results. Top managers may have data showing that performance has not been as good as it should have been, or has been more difficult to achieve than expected. They are looking for managers and employees to respond to the substandard performance and difficulties by coming up with some new ideas. They expect a special effort to be made to rectify the situation. In the absence of such responses, the top managers of the organisation may fear that complacency has set in. If the organisation has enjoyed a period of success prior to the disappointing results, then the complacency may be viewed as a natural consequence of previous success. Alternatively, it may be seen as reflecting a situation in which managers and employees are not really accountable to the public and are not motivated to perform at the required level.

CORPORATE HEALTH

Chief executives are concerned with the overall functioning of their organisations. But they have a special interest in how well it is working in a corporate sense. This means the extent to which all parts of the organisation are working in a co-ordinated way and with a single unity of purpose. This assessment has a number of dimensions: the top management team, management generally, teamworking, clarity, IT systems, and strategy.

The chief executives will weigh up the calibre of their own management team, with whom they share responsibility for the corporate management of the organisation. The chief executive considers the capability, energy, and loyalty of the individual members of his or her management team. Loyalty matters as much as capability when corporate health of the organisation is being assessed.

They will also make assessments about the whole body of managers in the organisation. Some obvious questions may be:

• Is there a rapid turnover of managers?
• Are managers too busy fire-fighting?

- Are relationships between managers and professionals constructive?
- Are management meetings talking shops or are decisions being made?

In some public services managers may have a professional background and have taken up their managerial roles with very little management training. The chief executive may well be concerned that the managerial rather than the professional perspective should be uppermost. They are increasingly concerned to see managers engaged in cross-boundary working. They want managers in different departments to talk directly to each other. They want managers to move across departmental boundaries to find skill and expertise if they do not exist in their own department. None of this spells an end to hierarchy—just an end to the belief that all co-ordination and resourcing have to be secured through the management line.

Chief executives may also be keen to see the existence of a corporate ethos of teamworking. They may look for tangible evidence of teamworking, knowing how easy it is for organisations to project a spirit of teamworking that has little basis in fact. They may also assess the extent to which operational interdependencies were used to structure teams properly, and how well individuals had been prepared, trained, and facilitated for teamworking.

Some, but by no means all, chief executives assess the degree of clarity or muddle in the organisation. They may have different ways of rectifying confusion and muddle, but the assumption is usually made that clarity is desirable. This clarity may be sought in terms of corporate visions or values or in terms of operational activities, responsibilities, and accountabilities. The thinking in recent years has often stressed the importance of the organisation having values, meaning that all the people in the organisation understand and share a set of values. It is reckoned that from such shared values come commitment and a focus on performance and quality.

Increasingly the corporate health of public services organisations depend on IT systems. Such systems are needed to ensure that core processes function smoothly. In universities and hospitals, for example, effective records systems are essential for keeping track of individuals. Local authorities need good IT systems for managing budgets and for service delivery. Government employment services, for example, need systems which match unemployed people to job vacancies. The functioning of these IT systems depends as much, if not more, on their operation by employees as it does on their technical specifications.

Chief executives, especially the ones who see themselves as the strategic leader of the organisation and the chief designer of strategies, will assess the organisation's strategic capacity. Is there, for instance, a strategic centre to the organisation? How good is the organisation at determining where it wants to go strategically? How strong is its ability to implement strategic developments? How well does the strategic centre deal with the controversy created by strategic change?

There is an overlap here with the assessment of corporate health. Chief executives may assess the consistency of strategies produced by the various units of the organisation, and may see their role as ensuring consistency among the strategies. Moreover, they may assess the strategies of units for their fit with corporate aims set out in corporate plans. Both of these are about developing a corporate approach to strategy.

FINANCIAL HEALTH

The new chief executive will without doubt assess the financial position of his or her new organisation, assessing income, costs, cash flow, etc., but also how well budgets are managed and co-ordinated.

The chief executive may assess the overall financial position in terms of the solvency or insolvency of the organisation. Insolvency can arise in a number of different ways. Provider organisations operating in the context of competitive tendering may run a deficit when the income from the client organisation is insufficient or is not efficiently claimed. Universities may run a deficit when income from student fees falls below projected levels and staffing levels exceed what is required. Training agencies may face a deficit when they fail to deliver central government programmes they had contracted to do. If these are not handled, organisations end up making people redundant and even, in some cases, may be closed down.

The assessment of costs will be critically important where there is a deficit problem. The assessment is made by comparison with costs in other organisations. A university will look at its costs compared to other universities. A hospital will look at its costs compared to other hospitals. And so on. Labour costs are often a high proportion of total costs. For example, modern universities may have over 60 per cent of their costs attributed to staff. Other costs include electricity, telephones, equipment, materials, travel and subsistence expenses, and so on. Many of the non-staff costs are difficult to control, so staff costs receive close attention. The assessment may also extend to the systems of controlling staff costs—how much control has the organisation got over the way in which labour costs are incurred? Are vacancies always filled or does the organisation have sound procedures for checking whether the funding for the post would be better used in some other way?

The assessment of financial health may address the future as well as the present. This involves looking at planned expenditures, costs, inflation trends, and forecasts of central government grants.

Managing and co-ordinating budgets properly is obviously crucial for a sound performance by the organisation. Sometimes the budget process is not properly managed and co-ordinated. The organisation may have lost control of its budgets. There may be sections or units of the organisation that have chronically overspent. This may have been covered by underspends in other areas. Nevertheless, overspends may indicate loose control rather than unanticipated costs or needs. It may represent, therefore, a distortion of the priorities established by elected politicians or senior managers. In some cases the budget formulation process has become so poor that top managers may then not even know how financial resources are actually being allocated. Consequently the assessment will no doubt take in the question of central control over financial management. A new chief executive will take a close look at how well the director of finance controls financial management and how well managers manage their own budgets. The finance system itself will come in for close scrutiny, including the software used in the financial system. The assessment may focus on how widely budgetary control is delegated and how suitable this amount of delegation is. In some public sector organisations, top managers have been keen on empowering line managers and have delegated substantial budgetary authority. Other public sector organisations have taken the view that this is not desirable and have wanted to keep budgetary control centralised. The popular thinking has been to delegate budgetary authority, but fear of costly mistakes has made some organisations slow to loosen the grip of the centre.

Even if budgets are well managed, top managers hope to increase organisational results by achieving better co-ordination of budgets. This may even be attempted with other public sector organisations or agencies where there is an overlapping legal mandate to deliver services.

PERFORMANCE HEALTH

A fundamental aspect of any assessment of the functioning of a public sector organisation these days is the assessment of its performance. The 1990s brought a new concern for planned and continuing improvements in performance by government. So, the chief executive of a public sector organisation looks to see whether performance is good and improving. This has become the most basic assessment of the health of the organisation. If performance is not improving, if results are not getting better, then there is a serious problem that needs addressing.

Performance and results can be assessed taking into account financial resources. This is about assessing value for money. So, are good results being achieved at a cost that is reasonable? The public sector organisation must have regard to its value chain (Porter 1985) in order to deliver to the public good value for the tax revenue spent on public services. This has led in part to a concentration on cutting costs and eliminating waste. This involves developing more focused activities and 'crisper' organisations. But cost management is only part of the drive to improve the value for money performance of public services.

All kinds of public sector organisations have been upgrading their performance. They have been under pressure to make substantial productivity gains. They have been pressurised to be more flexible. They have been encouraged to be more entrepreneurial. These demands for more performance have been transmitted in terms of requirements for more accountability through submitting planning documents and through increased auditing of activities and performance.

Increasingly the performance of the public sector organisation has been judged in terms that make sense from a consumer viewpoint rather than a professional one. In the health services, hospital performances are judged in terms of waiting lists and waiting times.

In schools the judgements are based on exam passes by students. These performance measures are chosen by politicians, but reflect the political judgement that public services need to be more accountable to the service users.

In recent years the evaluation of performance has been increasingly placed in a strategic framework. So, strategic goals are set, and from these are derived performance goals. Then the system of management is completed by a performance management system. The managers of public sector organisations have worked hard at setting up effective and rigorous performance management systems. They have invested time and effort in developing performance indicators and establishing the measurability of performance targets. Such performance management systems have been established at various levels: the whole organisation, operating units, and even individuals. The drive has been to align the efforts of individuals with the activities of units, and the activities of units with the strategic goals of the whole organisation. Some public sector managers have been approaching measurability issues by taking a leaf out of the book of private sector experiments. There have been trials of the balanced scorecard idea and the use of the business excellence model to support performance planning and measurement.

Some of the improvements in performance planning, measurement, and improvement have also benefited from the increased availability of comparative information that has resulted from central government requirements to report performance information. Hospitals, for example, can use comparative information to judge whether or not they are getting better or worse as compared to similar hospitals in their region. This official data has been supplemented in some cases by voluntary benchmarking clubs being set up by public sector organisations. For example, public sector leisure organisations may co-operate to produce performance data that they can then use to develop performance-planning systems.

The chief executive wishing to assess performance of his or her organisation can judge the adequacy of this performance in a variety of ways. Most obviously, the chief executive can look for gaps between actual performance and performance targets. A university may be judged to have a healthy performance when, for example, it recruits students in numbers set out as targets in performance plans. Another approach is to judge adequacy in relative terms. In other words, comparisons with similar organisations may be used to judge whether or not the organisation is performing satisfactorily, and whether changes over time are showing a positive trend.

Performance in terms of quality seemed to move up the agenda of public sector managers (and governments) only in the 1990s, after a decade of concentrating on managing costs and efficiency. Chief executives in public sector organisations have to worry increasingly about external quality audits. Universities may be audited for both the quality of their teaching and of their research. Local authority services may be inspected for the effectiveness and quality of what they do. Clinical effectiveness in health services has become a matter of public accountability in a way that it never was in the heyday of professional domination.

The assessment of quality may be assessed by chief executives reading the reports of inspections, reports analysing complaints, and specially commissioned qualitative research among service users.

Arguably, quality is still overlooked in assessments of organisational health by comparison with assessments of financial position and performance.

Probably as a result of the quality movement in the public sector, politicians and public sector managers are increasingly expressing an interest in continuous improvement. This may be seen as requiring a constant search for improvements, an attitude of never being satisfied, always challenging existing ways of doing things, and making lots of improvements over time. This commitment to continuous improvement can be seen as the essence of the public sector model of innovative organisations.

ADAPTABILITY: CHANGE, INNOVATION AND ENTREPRENEURIAL ACTION

Many public sector organisations have been moving beyond a cost management mentality. They have accepted that they have to do useful things for the public as well as reduce costs. This means making changes to realign organisations and activities with evolving public needs and priorities. Turning around the performance of poorly performing organisations sometimes involves tackling an organisational quagmire that causes every planned change to get bogged down. Chief executives making an assessment of their organisation may take as their initial benchmark whether managers are achieving any planned change at all.

But not all public sector organisations are in the poor category. Again they also have been going beyond the cost management mentality. Mediocre and middle-ranking organisations have been adding innovation to their toolbox. Innovation as much as cost management produces value for the public. Continuing to produce useful results always involves meeting new needs and meeting existing needs in new ways.

One of the main innovations attempted in recent years is the introduction of a seamless approach to public service delivery. This means working in partnership with public organisations with an overlapping mandate. Another is the redesign of public services that reduce dependency, build communities, and, generally, are less paternalistic.

The innovations being pursued are challenging public sector organisations to be good at both change and entrepreneurial action. The chief executive is typically interested in an organisation having an ability to act quickly on ideas, but this is tempered by a presumption that public sector organisations are like oil tankers, slow to get moving and slow to respond to changes of direction. Chief executives may assume that bureaucratic features indicate a lack of ability to act quickly. Capacity for entrepreneurial action is properly judged in terms of using and reusing resources to meet public needs in original and imaginative ways. Because of the bureaucratic legacy the capacity for entrepreneurial action may be judged instead by a willingness to take risks and do new things.

PUBLIC SATISFACTION

Public sector organisations are showing an increasing interest in measuring performance outcomes. Perhaps the easiest and most obvious measure of a performance outcome is public satisfaction with the service being provided. This is still often done in a rudimentary way, but the widespread interest in measuring service user satisfaction is one of the clearest examples of a major cultural change in the public sector.

There is a choice of emphasis in some managers' minds between an emphasis on performance in competitive terms and an emphasis on performance in meeting public needs. The former emphasis might be seen as organisations competing in the context of performance league tables for schools, hospitals, local authorities, and other public sector organisations. These league tables are constructed as data on actual performance against performance targets. Such league tables may be published and used by the public to pressurise for improvements. Of course, the league tables may also be used by central government and competition might be enforced through central government interventions. For example, those at the bottom of league tables might find themselves being inspected and scrutinised. Those at the tops of league tables might be rewarded by more freedoms from central controls. Competition might take the form of inter-organisational rivalry. This would take the form of the better performing organisations telling others how good they are and worse ones being embarrassed.

An emphasis on performance to meet public needs may be articulated by chief executives saying that they are primarily concerned with assessing how well their organisation is actually delivering the service to the public, and thus what matters is public satisfaction rather than performance league tables.

Perhaps in the future public sector managers will have an enhanced ability to manage for the public if they can make progress in measuring changes in performance against targets and changes in public satisfaction and then identifying the linkages between the two. In other words, when assessing the public sector organisation the top management team should be assessing both competitive performance against targets and public satisfaction. This need not be a matter of either–or.

Assessments of public satisfaction may be made on the basis of global measurements. But there may also be assessments of public satisfaction with specific aspects of public sector organisational performance. For example, to what extent is public satisfaction or dissatisfaction focused on the presence or absence of a seamless approach to service delivery?

ASSESSMENT PROCESS

The process of assessing and then improving the organisation involves acquiring data, making judgements, and then deciding how to improve the organisation's functioning. Acquiring data is largely a matter of listening to people and analysing written information. People will tell the chief executive and the top management team about the organisation. Documents of various kinds can be useful for finding out the background and history of the current situation, as well as providing data on financial and budgetary matters. However much data is obtained, there is then the separate process of making judgements about the performance of the organisation and its health in terms of the various aspects we have considered above. Finally, the chief executive must instigate action to bring about an acceptable level of functioning of the organisation.

A newly arrived chief executive (or other senior manager) may set up a formal programme of listening to people and collecting judgements. People throughout the organisation may be invited to meet with the chief executive on a one-to-one basis. The chief executive may offer to meet with groups of staff and visit them in their workplace. While some chief executives in the public sector may undertake a programme of listening when they first arrive, some have made such activity a permanent aspect of their role. One problem with such an approach, although highly commendable and very valuable to the chief executive, is that voluntary invitations to people in the organisation to provide information and their opinions will not necessarily produce all the information that is required from all parts of the organisation. Higher-level and more professional employees may be more ready to volunteer their views than front-line service delivery employees. So, 'listening programmes' need to be complemented by other information-gathering processes.

Of course, people in the organisation will not only provide data on its functioning and performance. They will also offer their own judgements of what the situation is and what needs doing. Top management, especially the chief executive, may be influenced by these judgements, but will have their own judgements, based on their own experiences of managing public sector organisations. In some matters the chief executive may accept what others are saying is an issue that needs attention. In other matters it may be more a matter of a combination of a range of people's perceptions and judgements. In some cases, the chief executive may think it right to form a judgement which is quite independent of all other people's assessments. Chief executives certainly give the impression of

knowing what kind of organisation they want, even if they are keen
to listen to others as well.

Some chief executives will consider how well the organisation is
functioning with their management team. Some will use an away
day or retreat with the management team, or with a specially
selected group of people. They work with their team or group to
develop an organisational improvement plan that identifies the
issues that need sorting out and the actions to address them. The
actions may be begun immediately, prior to the development of a
long-term strategic plan, but perfecting an organisation is likely to
be an ongoing concern of the chief executive and continue long after
the process of installing strategy has been launched.

IMPROVEMENT ACTIONS

The range of organisational improvement actions in the public
sector is wide. Some of the most common are outlined below.

Dialogue with politicians

If the relationship between elected politicians and managers of a
public sector organisation is poor then managers may consider
setting up a better relationship by increasing the frequency and
quality of dialogue.

Management development

Improvements in the calibre of management may be sought through
a whole variety of different methods. For example, organisations
may provide training courses for managers, and facilitated workshops to assist with the development of problem-solving and communication skills.

Employee development

Employee communication systems have been set up in a number of
public sector organisations to change cultures and instil corporate

values. The ultimate intention behind such developments may be to build understanding and commitment among employees.

The focus of employee communications may be guided by employee surveys. In some cases organisations have invested in a series of employee surveys to identify what employees are thinking and how attitudes are changing. The surveys may be full surveys of all employees in the organisation or sample surveys. In analysing the survey, the organisation may break down results for the different directorates, departments, or sections.

Corporate development

The growing criticism of the poor working relationships between departments in a single organisation has led to a variety of measures to improve corporate working.

One approach to developing corporate working is to establish corporate induction courses. These induction courses may be built around the idea of giving new employees some key 'messages'. The chief executive may contribute directly to the induction of new starters. Participation in the induction course may be made compulsory. The induction stresses the organisation's mission, its values, and what is expected of the new employee. The first impressions of the new employee may be seen as very important in establishing a corporate ethos.

Another idea that has been tried by many public sector organisations is the creation of a managers' forum. This can create a more corporate-minded body of managers. The forum does this by expanding the opportunities for managers to talk to each other. The forum may be scheduled for two hours every month or three or four times a year. When these take place, managers who might not otherwise meet face to face are brought together. Relationships are built and information flows more easily outside of the forum.

A third approach to building a corporate organisation is to draft managers and employees into project groups working on corporate issues. The idea is to develop corporate attitudes and habits by getting individuals to work alongside people from other departments, thereby developing more capacity to see issues in the round. A related idea is to allocate corporate responsibilities to senior managers who head up individual directorates and departments.

For these managers the experience of working on corporate matters tempers the sectionalism inherent in running a directorate or department.

One radical idea for addressing the need for corporate development has been to move responsibility for services between general managers in executive director roles. This may be done on a scheduled basis and with a degree of arbitrariness for the organisational architecture. Executive directors have found themselves responsible for services, and bundles of services, with which they have had little prior experience. This has been justified as being functionally effective because the executive directors are general managers who are using generic expertise and techniques. It has certainly produced more all-round executive directors. For the service-level managers it has been beneficial in fostering contact with service-level managers from other services, and it is alleged that this has been good for fostering lateral linkages within the organisation. Their director called meetings of service-level managers in their directorate, and relationships across service boundaries have formed, friendships developed, and dysfunctional departmental animosities abated. Understanding of the work of others has increased and with it mutual trust and respect have emerged.

Strategic capacity development

The growth of strategic management in the public sector means that new chief executives, who may be champions of strategic planning, may diagnose an organisation as too operational in its approach, and as lacking adequate capacity for strategic management. Actions to increase the capacity for strategic management include:

1. The creation of a more public focus for managers and employees by checking public opinion over time. Commissioning surveys by market research companies may do this. If this provides data on the organisation's effectiveness in achieving corporate goals, then the importance of strategic action may be underlined.
2. Funding strategic projects by the introduction of corporate budgets on top of budgets for service areas. This funding pays for the time of managers and others seconded from operational roles to work on projects.

3. Support for creativity to 'think outside of a box' and generate ideas for strategic innovation. Creativity and spontaneity are important as an antidote to bureaucratic conservatism, and thus key to creating the ground for strategic thinking within the organisation.

Actions such as surveying public opinion and setting up corporate budgets probably require no further comment. However, some ideas on how to encourage creativity may be useful. Providing access to corporate investment funds on a competitive base can facilitate creativity. Other mechanisms for encouraging creativity in strategic management include innovation and quality awards, benchmarking projects, partnerships and networks, and staff mobility policies (Meneguzzo & Lega 1999). These mechanisms work in different ways. Thus, awards stimulate change. Benchmarking leads to knowledge transfer through learning from others. Partnerships and networks lead to the exchange of knowledge. Staff mobility policies enable the transfer of know-how based on previous experience.

SUMMARY AND CONCLUSION

In this chapter we have looked at why assessing the healthy functioning of the organisation is important, what is assessed, and the improvement actions which may be taken to bring the organisation up to an adequate level of functioning. It was pointed out that managers could feel it is necessary to identify and begin addressing organisational issues and financial problems before they are able to turn to their strategic agenda.

One area of assessment is particularly important in many public sector organisations and this is the relationship of the top managers and politicians. It has been suggested that managers need to work on achieving a partnership with politicians in order that there is a good combination of the legitimacy of the politicians and the strategic goals of the manager. In addition the relationships with professionals are often critical. Good prospects for strategy exists when managers have an effective partnership with politicians, have the internal support of organisational constituencies (professionals), and support of the public. In the absence of these things—especially the partnership with politicians—the organisation is not ready for strategic change. Politicians are in the driving seat because they have the democratic legitimacy and also control the resources that top managers need to pursue strategies.

The fundamental need of managers for the support of elected politicians may explain why organisational issues have to be managed before strategic change can be attempted. If issues (such as financial or budgetary ones) are not handled effectively and prompt-ly, politicians may lose faith in the managers. They are then unable to gain democratic legitimacy for strategic change and may be refused the resources they need.

3
Paying Attention to Politicians

INTRODUCTION

Public sector organisations have a very important stakeholder—the government of the country. Public sector organisations have largely needed government because it provided funding. Other revenue was obtained by fees and charges for services, and from other sources. This has provided a powerful incentive for the managers who lead public sector organisations to think about what politicians want and expect, what politicians think about the priorities their organisations should be pursuing, and what perceptions the politicians had about how well the organisations were performing.

Public services organisations also pay attention to the views of the public in general and their service users in particular. This may be based on a public service ethic, which has emerged from an American study as an important motivation for innovation (Holzer & Callahan 1998). For example, universities may not only concern themselves with the needs of their students, but also their local, regional, and national communities. They may feel they have a responsibility to respond to the needs of society generally. But it is not only a public service ethic that explains this concern for the views of the public. It is bound to be, in part, because politicians may pay attention to public views and then make changes in laws, policies, and budgetary allocations that have impacts on public service organisations. In other words, it is the politicians who form the executive in government that are most important to organisational leaders.

National politicians have some importance for all public sector organisations. Local government organisations also have locally elected politicians, who have been elected by local communities to act as their representatives, and to provide a democratically elected executive for the organisations. The top managers of such organisations may have a lot of contact with the elected politicians who control the executive decision making of their organisation. They may have many opportunities to observe them and listen to their views. They may spend time discussing the politicians, speculating on their priorities and appraising how they should be responding to the demands of the politicians.

The process of understanding and paying attention to politicians can be a difficult one at times. For example, politicians at different levels or within the same political oversight bodies can have different political agendas. It cannot be assumed that there is a clear and coherent political will on all issues affecting the functioning of the organisation.

THE IMPORTANCE OF THE POLITICIANS

Senior managers in the public sector need to be aware of priorities of the politicians who direct and influence their organisations. A major reason for managers to work at ensuring that they understand political priorities is that they form a link in the chain of a democratic process. The public elects politicians to represent them and pursue their interests and aspirations. The public is able to do this because political parties present their intentions in political manifestos and the public is able to consider these and vote for the party that comes closest to reflecting its concerns. On this basis it is important that the intentions of the politicians are then expressed in laws, policies, and budgetary decisions and that these are then implemented by public service organisations.

If the top managers properly understand what the politicians are trying to achieve and what matters, then they can more effectively translate what they have to do to manage the organisation in accord with the political will. It may help to illuminate the processes of strategic change in the public sector to think in terms of managers taking the policies of politicians and turning them into strategies. 'What is, from the point of view of the organization, a strategy is for others an intelligible set of policies and a new vision of the purpose and legitimacy of governmental action in a particular area' (Heymann 1987, p. 184). This way of looking at the relationship between policy and strategy may be reconciled with a view that strategy is displacing policy. 'There is', said Pettigrew and his colleagues, 'increasing interest in the public sector in moving from a focus on "policy" to one of "strategy" (implying a greater concern with securing action around the espoused policies)' (Pettigrew et al. 1992, p. 19). This increasing interest reflects the approach of politicians to getting more results. They have been encouraging and requiring the use of strategic management to increase both performance and accountability. The politicians still have their political objectives and their policies, but they want to see these expressed in strategic plans and strategies. Managers have thereby been given more responsibility for the success of the public sector.

There is a substantial proportion of managers in the public services who have a commitment to democracy. They interpret their role as being one of the links in the chain which ensures that the public's wishes and the political mandate of victorious political parties are realised through the functioning of the organisations they manage. This might also be described as an aspect of a public service ethic among managers.

There are other reasons for the need to be aware of politicians' intentions and priorities. For example, such awareness is important for successful action by managers in handling budgets and coping with official inspections and audits. Understanding the politicians' priorities is obviously important when bids are made to increase budgetary allocations that are under the control of the politicians. Inspections and audits are used to hold those who direct and manage public sector organisations accountable. There is a need, therefore, for senior managers to understand priorities and concerns of politicians to ensure that the organisations they manage can demonstrate compliance with official requirements.

In some cases, where the politicians have a management role in the organisation—as they have had in UK local government—then senior managers work hard at understanding the politicians because they need to have effective working relations with them if they are to do their own job. The chief executive of a local authority will spend a lot of time building an effective relationship with politicians, especially the political leaders among the elected representatives. This is likely to be seen as the top priority for the chief executive. If they fail to establish this working relationship their chances of succeeding in their responsibility to implement strategy effectively will be minimal. This is a fundamental aspect of the personal credibility of top management in a public service organisation—have they got an effective working relationship with the politicians that matter? Have they got the kind of effective working relationship that can usually deliver the political support the managers need to succeed with strategic changes?

Getting political support is an axiomatic principle of public sector management (Heymann 1987). Wise top managers know that getting this support depends on managers fitting into the politicians' agenda, and not expecting the politicians to fit into the manager's agenda. There is a need to be seen by politicians as working on the politicians' agenda at all times. The chief executive, therefore, secures political backing by proposing changes that are consistent with what the politicians want to achieve. The politicians may then act as the sponsor of the idea being championed by management. The politicians make a big difference to the implementation of changes, providing they have decided that this is something that should happen.

The support of the politician is needed if management is to be able to act as leaders of the public sector organisation. Leadership has been distinguished from management. Leaders enjoy an ability to direct employees because the latter consent to follow. In the absence of leadership a manager's orders may be ignored when their actions cannot be monitored or sanctioned. But how do top managers become leaders? One answer is that a public sector organisation depends on elected politicians for resources, authority, and prestige and this will be more likely to be forthcoming if the organisation is meeting the elected politician's objectives. The organisation may be more likely to meet these objectives if it acts in a co-ordinated and focused way that is effective in achieving organisational goals that will deliver the overall political objectives. If a top manager is effective in securing the requisite resources, authority, and prestige, the organisation's employees may be more willing to accept the leadership of the top manager. And if they accept this leadership, then the top manager is more able to deliver goals in line with political objectives, which results in more resources, authority, and prestige from the elected politicians. In other words, strong leaders can deliver what politicians want because they can influence and control the organisation, and they are able to influence and control the organisation because of the political response when the organisation delivers what the elected politicians want.

If top management and politicians fail to develop a working relationship the result will usually be a dysfunctional organisation.

THE ELECTORAL CYCLE

Most senior managers in public sector organisations understand the importance of the electoral cycle. For one thing, the electoral cycle is accompanied by swings in party politics, and thus changes of political party in control of the executive machinery. Public sector managers are aware that as party fortunes fluctuate they have to adapt to different political agendas. When there is a change of political power in government the managers have also got to be aware of the extra difficulties this entails in establishing an effective working relationship with politicians. An incoming political administration may not trust the top managers appointed during the office of a previous political administration. They will have to work very hard to build the trust of the politicians in their ability to work to a new political agenda. This trust is essential if there is going to be confidence in the top managers.

Because of the electoral cycle, top managers may feel that politicians have a short-term horizon. They may even feel under pressure from this to do things that have a quick and visible impact, at minimal cost, and with minimal political risk:

> Battles over the public's reaction to a government agency and its programs carried out by spirited political partisans in the daily press and in their periodic campaigns, occur in a realm where appearances are political realities, where detailed justifications are impossible or ineffective, and where explanations may never catch up with accusations. It is very much the job of the manager of a government agency to attend to appearances whenever he is dealing with matters of agency vulnerability (Heymann 1987, pp. 48–9).

Some managers may think that politicians are too concerned with impressing the public that they can get results because they want to be re-elected at the next round of elections. But many top managers are not necessarily critical of this short-term mindset. They accept that this is inevitable in a public sector organisation—they are in a 'political organisation'.

The political pressure on top managers to ensure things happen and that the public can see that things are happening can become heightened in some political cycles. In the 1970s when social democratic governments around the world were faltering, incoming new right politicians came into political power with a reforming zeal. In the 1990s, the reinventing or modernising government agenda has brought an influx of younger politicians who are in a hurry to shake things up and get things moving. There is a strong desire by the politicians to make their mark on public sector organisations and the way they work.

This state of affairs can create an adverse response from some managers. They accuse the politicians of wanting change for change's sake, and climbing on the innovation bandwagon. They may accuse politicians of driving changes to advance their political careers. They say that bringing about highly visible changes is the way politicians gain a reputation and rise up the ranks of the political world. It may also be suspected that such jaundiced views are defensive attitudes and designed to discount the democratic legitimacy of the politicians' demands for change by public sector managers.

It is true that innovation became more fashionable in both the private and public sectors during the 1990s. Politicians are not immune to such fashions. They want to be seen as innovative, which means supporting initiatives for joined-up government, public–private partnerships, and getting in touch with the community—being 'pathfinders' for reinventing government. However, this fashionable idea of innovation may also be seen in the public sector context as about responding to a crisis in the relationship between the public and the public sector organisation (Corrigan & Joyce 1997). In this case, innovation may be part of a movement of renaissance, in which a new alignment is established between public needs and public services. However necessary such a period of realignment is, the consequence for managers and employees in the public sector is undoubtedly a rise in the level of uncertainty and risk. For the politicians the change is a political change that they feel has been legitimated at the ballot box.

Such periods of intense politically induced change offer the chief executives of public sector organisations some obvious choices. Do they keep their own head down and ensure their own organisation keeps a low profile, hoping the change will blow itself out? Do they make sufficient concession to the political agenda for change that they are moving at the speed of most other public sector organisations? By doing so they may hope to avoid drawing down the wrath of politicians, but at the same time they hope not to be in the vanguard of change taking the biggest risks. Or do they commit themselves to being adventurous and show that they want to embrace the changes being sought by politicians? Do they make public statements about their willingness to be in the forefront of the innovations the politicians want? It may be surprising, but there are many public sector chief executives who will take the bold option and seek to be a leader in terms of innovations which governments want.

POLITICAL MANAGEMENT

Contemporary discussions of public sector management often tacitly assume the traditional view of public administration as a point of departure that says that politicians make policies and administrators implement them. In recent years it is assumed this division is breaking down:

> In modern society with all its new problems and opportunities (due to complexity, dynamics and diversity), the traditional Weberian distinction between the political system and the administrative apparatus can no longer be contained. In societies where policy making of governmental agencies and their clientele groups, public managing is more and more 'political' in the traditional sense. Also the civil servant sets the agenda, promotes or hampers consensus, wins social support and makes bargains (Kooiman & van Vliet 1993, p. 65).

Public sector managers are not able, so much, to say they only implement the politicians wishes; they are required to think about what needs to be done, not only how things should be done. In this sense we have a new 'political' management—paid officials who do not simply implement the will of the politicians.

The new political management has to concern itself with analysing the situation the public sector organisation finds itself in and planning how it can best deliver results. It still works at ensuring the organisation does what the politicians want, but it is involved to a much higher degree than ever before in interacting with the public and helping politicians to understand what is needed. This produces a rough match between the public's needs and the politicians' priorities.

It is worth saying that, however much the realities of political management deviate from the formal presuppositions of representative democracy, there is a lot of genuine commitment among senior public sector managers to being part of a democratic process. This means that there exists a desire to act on the basis of the wishes of politicians and to serve the public.

In fact, in many public sector organisations, the top managers experience being directed and driven by the politicians. They know they are managing as part of a political and not managerialist agenda. They experience their relationship with politicians in terms entirely consistent with the idea that politicians are in control. They will describe political leadership as very strong and very clear on its approach to specific issues.

In some public sector organisations this political control over senior managers is sufficiently loose for the chief executives to feel that they are not accountable to specific politicians or political oversight bodies. In this situation the chief executive may seem a fairly autonomous individual, and left to his or her own political devices. However, this is more likely to be a situation in which political control has been mediated by mechanisms such as funding agencies and quality audit systems.

ADVISING POLITICIANS

Senior public sector managers have an important role in advising politicians about the different ways of achieving the ends they have resolved on. The advice may cover the allocation and use of resources to obtain the best value for the public. It may cover the selection of the best operational arrangements. Whether to employ managers and employees to provide services in house, whether to externalise activities through contracting out, whether to set up public–private partnerships, and so on. Managers may also need to give advice on the standards of efficiency, service quality, public satisfaction, and continuous improvement that can be reasonably expected on the basis of benchmarking and other studies. Senior managers sometimes have a role in locating and helping politicians access expert advice, and do not always have to be the source of all expertise themselves.

Chief executives and senior managers need to meet with politicians frequently, formally and informally, so that the process of giving advice becomes part of a natural and easy process of ongoing dialogue. Many of the discussions in such a dialogue between politicians and managers can be centred on an evolving issue agenda. In these discussions each of the top issues may be gone through, the current approach examined, and managers test out through discussions whether the politicians feel that sufficient progress is being made, or whether the time has come to try a new approach.

Senior public sector managers often define their responsibility in this process of dialogue as ensuring that the politicians have sound advice before they take a decision. This shows that they recognise that the politicians are in charge, and that their job is to support effective political decision making. The advisory role of the public sector manager can nevertheless be a very influential one—providing there is mutual trust and respect between the politician and the manager. There is also a requirement for the politician and the manager to understand the boundary between their roles. Managers may understand their job is to advise and thus enable the politician to make effective decisions regarding the overall direction of the organisation. But managers are also keen that politicians should understand that managers usually need political support for action, and only rarely want the direct involvement of politicians in management action. In this sense, managers see themselves as running the organisation with the help of politicians, even though managers fully recognise that the politicians provide the overall direction of the organisation.

DELIVERING WHAT THE POLITICIANS WANT

Chief executives of public sector organisations know that they have got to deliver the political aims of the politicians. This is especially the case when politicians have made very clear promises to the electorate and believe that the results at the polls will depend on how well the public sector organisations have achieved the targets which have been set.

In some organisations the politicians will have specified policies and the chief executive develops a statement of strategic direction and associated strategic goals to ensure that these policies are achieved. In other cases, the politicians will have produced strategic visions and maybe even goals, and they will look to the managers to deliver in terms of their implementation. Such things vary in part because politicians differ in their attitudes to strategic management and in their judgements about their role in strategy. But managers are generally aware that they must achieve what it is the politicians wish to achieve.

The chief executive, who is often the most acutely aware of the need to serve the politicians, must impress on managers throughout the organisation the need to pay attention to the wishes and priorities of politicians. In doing so, the chief executive needs to recognise that middle managers and front-line managers are more preoccupied with day-to-day operational issues, and have to be convinced to seek to address the political imperatives through day-to-day decisions and issues.

PUTTING POLICIES INTO OPERATION

The policies made by politicians may accumulate over a long period of time and form a complex and even confusing body of policies. In these circumstances public sector managers may find themselves reminding politicians of what their policies are and explaining how they are acted upon. If there are new policies, the senior managers of a public sector organisation have to work out the practicalities of implementation. This involves thinking through operational changes and setting new objectives and budgets for operational management.

This can be quite a stretching process. Politicians obviously want managers not only to make sure things happen and things get done, they also want a level of performance that brings electoral dividends. Politicians are increasingly asking managers to achieve radical improvements in results, to create outstanding productivity levels, and engineer innovations. More than one public sector organisation has espoused the aim of being the best. Chief executives and senior managers may worry whether the expectations of what they can do are too ambitious.

However, many public sector chief executives are ambitious in terms of the performance of their organisations and are self-critical of the management of the public sector in the past. They see considerable opportunity to implement policies in line with political expectations, providing that systems of performance measurement are enhanced. They are confident that measuring performance and management information systems can be developed beyond the rudimentary state that has been widespread in the public sector. In any case, in many different countries public sector organisations are having performance measurement introduced as a matter of public policy. This is creating the possibility of politicians monitoring much more closely how their legal mandates and policies are being implemented.

PARTNERSHIPS BETWEEN POLITICIANS AND MANAGERS

There are now chief executives and senior managers in the public sector who want to develop a new kind of relationship with politicians which they describe in terms of 'working in partnership'. This appears to mean that as managers they expect to have the chance to debate ideas and views on issues with the politicians. They do not want just to be told by politicians what to do. And to the extent that managers have developed strategic directions and plans to achieve the aims of the politicians, they look for support from politicians in promoting them. Although not an equal relationship, they want more dialogue and give and take. This might mean that they expect politicians to be receptive to suggestions made by managers and not just expect them to be implementing the decisions of the politicians. But, to reiterate, the managers are looking for a degree of receptivity to their ideas and expertise; they are not looking to usurp the leadership role of the politicians.

This requires a change of political culture and an end to an administrative culture among paid officials. It requires both the politicians and the managers to feel comfortable with increased give and take.

One key to making this change is the preparation by managers for the strategy formulation process. Managers need to ensure that they are very clear about the politicians' priorities and concerns. And they need to make it clear to the politicians that any strategic goals and operational goals that are subsequently formulated by management will be closely based on these priorities and political concerns.

Managers can work on preparing for strategy formulation by suggesting that joint bodies of politicians and managers carry out strategic reviews together, when they look at how well the public sector organisation is performing against targets, and seek explanations for any discrepancies. In the context of such strategic reviews, managers may also gain enormously from the opportunities of listening to politicians talk about their perceptions of political trends and what are the limits of politically feasible action by the organisation. In return, managers are able to provide politicians with information on operational and community developments and issues that arise in the course of organisational activities. The managers get some feedback (not enough) from employees who deliver the services, and also from the public (sometimes through public consultation exercises). One of the benefits of such a strategic review is clearly the mutual education provided through interactions and dialogue focused on strategic goals and performance.

SUMMARY AND CONCLUSIONS

In a democratic system the strategic goals of managers are shaped by the political objectives of elected politicians. We must underline the extra requirements of a strategic leadership role in the public sector by virtue of the importance of the pluralistic system of interests both inside and outside most public sector organisations. The political system itself is pluralistic even in terms of the party political rivalry between majority parties that may control the legislature and the executive, and minority parties that compete for political power. This means goals and plans may need to be shaped taking account of the wisdom of the managers appearing to be the agents of the majority party, or a neutral and professional administration, or self-conscious mediators between the political parties (Heymann 1987).

4
Issue Management

INTRODUCTION

Chief executives in public sector organisations have had to develop capabilities for issue management. This appears to be the result of major changes in the organisational environment. As the challenges to traditional public sector activities have built up, top managers have found themselves confronting resource issues, community issues, and organisational issues. It is no longer possible to see the job of managing in terms of simple planning and controlling.

THE NEED TO MANAGE ISSUES

The pressures to identify, monitor, and manage issues are partly political in nature. Politicians have been articulating concern over issues and expressing commitment to handling issues. The politicians are probably the key stakeholder group in the current public sector. If they feel strongly that something needs to be done on an issue then managers feel motivated to respond. These issues may be big ones and politicians may state ambitious and stretching targets for tackling them. The politicians may be acting on the basis of political calculations or on the basis of their beliefs and principles. But, either way, the need to deal with issues has become more important because politicians are demanding that public sector organisations should address issues.

Political leaders may have their own subjective influences when articulating issues requiring action, but similar resource, community, and organisational issues appear to be on the agenda of many public sector organisations. And, by and large, top public sector managers take on board these issues, and ensure that there is a management response to the political will of the government or the politicians on the appropriate political oversight body.

The politicians also create pressures and inducements to act on the key issue agendas they identify. They may, for example, offer additional funding on a competitive basis to public sector organisations that address selected issues. They develop audit and inspection services. They create legal duties to act in desired ways.

For example, there has been an issue about the quality of university education in the UK, partly fuelled by fears of the impact of increased student numbers and changes in the real level of public subsidy for each student. The issue of teaching and research quality in the universities has been made a concern for university management by the system of assessment that produces teaching rating and research rating. University managers tend to be highly conscious of the need to manage quality even while they have set ambitious growth targets for their institutions.

But public sector managers do not only become concerned about issues because they are forced to do so. As we noted in Chapter 3, there are public sector managers who see themselves as a link in the democratic process, and thus accept the right of governments and politicians to identify issues that managers should then strive to address. Governments may, for example, identify a set of themes for public services leaders and others to work on. Especially in a period when new concepts of political governance and community leadership have become important in many different countries, these themes are seen as creating an agenda for societal or community problem solving. Leaders in the public, private, and voluntary sectors are expected separately and together to mobilise resources and action to solve the problems identified by these themes (Osborne & Gaebler 1992). Consequently, themes articulated by governments can be very rapidly installed in issue agendas of public sector managers.

Dealing with new issues, rather than simply perfecting the delivery of existing services, has been given a political rationale by some politicians and public sector managers, who are concerned about falling electoral turnout by citizens. One proposition is that the public is becoming apathetic about voting because it sees politics as irrelevant to their lives. Consequently, it can be argued, if politicians can get public sector organisations to address the issues that do concern the public, perhaps there will be a renaissance in voting behaviour. This concern about citizen apathy may be seen as most acute in the case of young people. If the public sector organisations just carry on doing what they have always done, and do not adapt their activities to address the new issues, it may be feared that the young will not acquire the habits of democracy.

As more and more public sector organisations spend time surveying and consulting the public, the awareness of issues for the public must potentially increase among public sector managers. Then managers may feel some urgency to deal with issues that they have found to be of concern to the public. This is particularly so where managers have a public sector ethos and feel a general duty to serve the public and respond to its needs and concerns.

The search for issues of concern to the public has also become a factor in issue management. More and more top public sector managers want to know what the public thinks. More and more of them are interested in empathising with the public. So they are organising surveys of the public's views about, for example, quality of life issues. They are interested in knowing what members of the public feel about the issues. They are becoming interested in forms of public consultation that allow more in-depth data to be obtained. Thus, alongside telephone surveys, public sector managers are commissioning focus group research. This implies a sizeable mindset shift by managers. They are realising that they can only know they are serving the public better if they are addressing issues of concern to the public and doing so in a way that produces solutions satisfactory to the public. The public's perspective is becoming established as the bottom line of public sector performance.

In addition to the considerations above, there is a socio-political analysis of the importance of public sector managers responding to issues. This analysis draws attention to the emergence of a significant section of society that is excluded from many of the benefits of modern life. This section of society is reckoned to be suffering from multiple problems, each of which can be designated as an issue. Inasmuch as the problems of this excluded minority could spill over and affect the rest of society, there is an instrumental as well as a moral argument for public sector organisations ensuring that they are helping with these problems.

The socially excluded section of society is often seen as located primarily in big cities and in areas of the cities that are marked by community breakdown. The portrayal of these areas may seem a little stereotyped, but they are characterised by transient populations, concentrations of ethnic minorities, language difficulties, fear of crime, high unemployment, low educational levels, poor incomes, poor health, and so on. The general assumption is that the public sector must address these issues in these communities urgently, otherwise community breakdown will accelerate and create an unacceptable situation.

The socio-political analysis may be extended to include pessimistic assessments of the community's capacity for taking care of itself. This may be used to argue the case for the public sector to tackle these issues by community development work. It is presumed that successful community development will create individuals, families, and neighbourhoods that are resourceful and independent. People in the community will, it is said, help each other. If this does not happen, then the ability of the public sector to provide paid staff to do this caring and helping will be completely inadequate.

THE NEED TO MANAGE ORGANISATIONAL ISSUES

Some issue management occurs because of the importance to public sector managers of ensuring the survival and success of their organisations. The experience of a new chief executive arriving at an organisation to find it in a state of chaos and threatened by the poor financial management of the previous management is by no means unique. The issues threatening survival of the organisation may call for emergency action immediately, or there may be an extended period of fire-fighting just to keep the organisation afloat. Years ago the view may have been taken that public sector organisations were immortal, but years of reorganisations, retrenchments, and internal markets have long since added the word 'survival' to the vocabulary of the public sector manager. In consequence, the chief executive may have only one thought in mind when engaged in issue management—survival. The chief executive may think in terms of first handling the issues in the fight to survive, then creating some stability, and then hopefully starting to build the success of the organisation.

This survival motivation is not simply the natural desire of an individual to perpetuate an organisation in which they have a career stake. Chief executives in the public sector have and feel responsibilities towards the people who use the services of the organisation and the people who are employed providing those services. Chief executives will sometimes confide that the threat of job losses and the inability to reassure employees about job security weigh heavily on their minds.

Then there is the competition motivation. Many chief executives do feel that their organisation is competing against other public sector organisations. This can be seen in the university sector. It can be seen in the health sector. Even local authorities, which have defined geographical boundaries, have competed for funding, recognition, and status even if they have not directly competed for service users. This means that chief executives will identify organisational issues that are important because they are damaging the ability of their organisation to compete. Universities, hospitals, local authorities, and other organisations in the public sector will identify, for example, issues such as poor facilities that impede the quality and efficiency of services. Under-investment in proper facilities holds back chief executives trying to establish their organisations as competitive and innovative.

Resource and organisational issues have to be addressed even when there is an optimistic and bold management team leading an organisation. Ambition carries a risk, and especially the risk of taking up a strategic position that outstrips capacity. Therefore, resource and organisational issues may need to be tackled so that management is in a position to set ambitious but realistic goals and performance targets.

Issue management can be of critical importance to the chief executive preparing the ground for strategic leadership. A vital resource for strategic leadership is trust in top management. If a public sector organisation has had a very bruising experience of poor management, and mismanagement, then a new chief executive has quite a battle to renovate a level of trust in the leadership of the organisation. The research on the British National Health Service by Pettigrew et al. (1992) brings out this point quite clearly in their discussion of events at Rainhill Hospital (England). They report:

Thus staff were often reluctant to accept its [closure of the hospital's] legitimacy. There is still disbelief in parts of the organization that total closure will take place, fuelled by continuing upgrading work and by the absence of visible new alternative services. Closure has been mooted for more than 20 years, but never actualized; and there is a scepticism about management's ability to deliver (Pettigrew et al. 1992, p. 163).

It will be very difficult to expect such an organisation to react with anything but a wait and see attitude to the announcement of a strategic blueprint for the long-term development of the organisation. The new management must build its credibility. It needs a track record of successful management. Issue management can be very helpful in this respect. Each issue solved should engender trust among managers and employees.

RESOURCE ISSUES

From a strategic planning perspective, resource issues are tied to the feasibility of strategic change. Top managers look at their strategic goals and the strategic actions planned, and then make an assessment of the availability of the resources for accomplishing these actions. In the context of ambitious strategic goals, the availability of resources has loomed large as an issue in the public sector.

Money is by no means the only resource that is needed for strategic action, but there has been a big preoccupation with it among many public sector managers. There has been a widespread perception that budgetary allocations have meant that funding has become more of a constraint. Some public sector managers complain about constant pressures on budgets year after year, and the rarity of a growth budget. This may be seen as having a direct consequence for the rationing of public services. In social services, for example, the rationing process may be managed by the application of eligibility criteria. Managers express concern that members of the public experience increasing difficulties in accessing services as eligibility criteria are drawn tighter and tighter. In some parts of the public sector—such as health services—the financial constraints have been partly driven by the increased expensiveness of inputs (e.g. technology, drugs). It is also sometimes suggested that budgetary pressures have been exacerbated by a growth in consumerism in the public sector that has put additional pressure on budgets as a result of rising public expectations. As public sector managers have wrestled with the problems of financial constraints, they have considered ways of reducing demand through preventative work (Osborne & Gaebler 1992) as well as opportunities for increasing income through charging. These possible solutions have side effects that sometimes concern public sector managers. Preventative work needs resourcing and arguments for budget allocations may seem less urgent for such work than requests for funding to provide services for immediate needs. Charging for public services raises anxieties about equity issues, because the people who can afford charges may not be as needy as those who would be deterred by charges.

The resource issues faced by some chief executives can be quite acute. Hospitals, local authorities, and other organisations can find themselves with enormous budget deficits of millions of pounds. In the face of such deficits, and in the absence of extra government funding, the chief executives of such organisations have to find large-scale savings within their current operations. (Even more savings have to be found if the organisations are developing new activities or services while managing cutbacks.) Major cost reduction programmes may have to be used to find savings of the order of 5 per cent of the budget. This is the main way they can turn a budget deficit into a surplus. Management overhead costs may be targeted to bear the brunt of cost reductions. For as long as possible organisations may try to protect front-line services from cutbacks. Such experiences have a profound effect on the attitudes of managers and employees in public sector organisations. They may cause managers to become very focused on value for money because revenue is becoming a scarcer resource. Some organisations may develop tunnel vision as continuing budgetary constraints train managers in habits and ways of thinking which are about managing to keep on doing what it has always done. The positive side of this is the ingenuity used by managers to maintain services despite the reductions of revenue. They change staffing, service delivery systems, control procedures, and many other things. But in the process they cease to think about how to adapt the organisation to do new things.

One other effect that such experiences have is to foster an interest in income generation. For example, universities that are largely funded out of tax revenue start to rethink their attitudes to revenue.

Instead of assuming that all increases in funding must come from central government, the top managers begin to encourage university staff to generate income. This causes some soul searching, and excessively commercial motives may be spurned. But, nevertheless, there is an increased openness to widening the funding base.

To sum up, there is an increasing concern in public sector organisations with balancing the books by cost management and income generation, and in this climate there is a much stronger appreciation of the need to focus on value for money in using tax revenue to provide public services. The financial constraints over many years have had a major cultural effect on managers and employees in the public sector.

DEMOCRACY ISSUES

The public sector may have taken its democratic credentials for granted 30 or 40 years ago, but public sector organisations of all kinds worry about their responsiveness and accountability to the public. Government organisations in particular may feel that they may rely too much on the electoral process as their way of linking to the public. More and more are making attempts to go further in engaging with citizens. This is at both the community and the neighbourhood level.

The relationship with citizens is not the only democracy issue in the public sector. There are tiers of government, and elected politicians exist at many levels of the political structure. The electoral process confers legitimacy on all of them, and thus there is scope for disagreements between levels of government. In the case of Europe, there can be conflicts between European, national, regional, or local levels. In the UK, especially between 1979 and 1997, there was a degree of tension between national and local government. National government worried about irresponsible action by local politicians, and local government accused the national government of being bossy and throwing its weight around. It has often been argued by local politicians that the centralising tendency (at least until 1997) was undermining local democracy. Poor voter turnouts in UK local government can either be seen as weakening the legitimacy of local politicians, or as evidence of public apathy caused by the emasculation of local government.

Some degree of tension between levels of government is bound to exist. There is obvious scope for differences between levels of government in terms of revenue and expenditure, the handling of social issues, party political matters, and much more. The amount of tension does, however, vary, and does so in part depending on the complexion and character of the politicians.

Democracy is a way of handling collective decision making and differences in society. Society is always changing and evolving. Democratic structures as well as the issues being handled by democracy also change and evolve. There have been academic speculations on the long-term developments in structures (Bohret 1993), but managers in public sector organisations are facing restructuring and reorganisations brought about by reforms and innovation to improve governance structures. Throughout Europe over the last 30 years the regions have become more important. In Scotland and Wales we could well be seeing lots of new issues of a regional nature being given more prominence as a result of the modernisation of democratic arrangements.

Regionalism is starting to develop in England as well. This raises issues for chief executives and senior managers in public sector organisations. They may want to ensure that their organisation has a voice in the new regional forums that emerge. More and more top managers may find themselves thinking about how their organisation's operations will be affected and what other implications there might be as a result of regionalism. This depends in part on the nature of the new regionalism in the UK. If regionalism is marked by greater partnership working, then public sector organisations in each region may be spending more time and effort on cross-boundary management. If regional levels of government are primarily strategic in nature, and work by enabling, then public sector organisations may put effort into getting their voice heard at regional level so as to advance their own strategic agendas. For example, city councils may be in some rivalry to position themselves as regional centres. If the regional level has some say in resource allocation, then public sector organisations will be busy negotiating for their share of the budgetary allocations. Whatever the eventuality, the arrival of regionalism will mean another dimension to the activities of top managers in large public sector organisations.

COMMUNITY ISSUES

Whole sets of new issues—community issues—have come to the
fore in recent years. And given the growing interest in the United
States, in Britain, and elsewhere in a more co-ordinated approach
by public sector organisations, these issues are not the provinces of
a single public sector organisation operating in isolation. In 1997
the United States Congress was told by Susan Kladiva, a general
accounting officer examiner, that how well federal agencies met
their strategic goals depended on how well they co-ordinated their
efforts (*The Daily Fed*, 25 July 1997). In 1998 Frank Dobson, the
UK's Health Secretary, required health and social services to work
in partnership on the same set of priorities as part of the programme of modernisation.

Issues being tackled by public sector organisations include many
of the following problems:

* Environmental pollution
* Traffic congestion (in town centres, on motorways)
* Recycling (which is tricky in part because of the costs imposed
  on the business community)
* Economic development and regeneration
* Town centre development (in part a response to retailing devel-
  opments outside of towns)
* Unemployment
* Community safety, and the fear of crime
* Drugs
* Pockets of poverty and disadvantage
* Discrimination against people from multi-ethnic communities
* Homelessness
* Disability issues
* Ill health prevention
* Elderly people
* Social exclusion issues
* Asylum seekers (who put pressures on our social services, and
  budgets)
* Quality of life issues

The idea of partnership working has become a hot topic among
leaders of public sector organisations. In thinking strategically
about any or all of these issues, chief executives are likely to say that

their ability to deliver solutions depends on their organisation's relationships with other organisations.

ORGANISATIONAL ISSUES

There may be organisational issues. Some of these will concern the treatment and remuneration of employees (e.g. equal opportunities, single-status employment conditions for blue-collar and white-collar employees). Some will concern service delivery. Prior to the 1980s concern for service delivery was embedded in professional cultures. Now it has become a focus for public sector management. There is general talk in management circles about setting and attaining quality standards in services. This may be a result of several different processes. First, political agendas can be expressed directly in management aims to raise standards. Politicians have prioritised improvements in education and health to achieve enhanced quality of life and economic performance. In this way, political concerns have a direct link to management issues. The politicians' concerns for quality of life and better economic performance may lead to demands for more effective public services that may be expressed in terms of outcomes, as in the commitment to raise, and to continue raising, standards in education. Second, quality standards may be an issue for an organisation because it is trying to deliver increasing value for money without sacrificing quality. For example, many British universities have expanded student numbers over a relatively short period of time but have worried about maintaining the quality of what they do. They have talked about the need to pay attention to the quality of both teaching and research. This has been accompanied in some cases by changing perceptions among university managers about the function of a university and the conditions for obtaining public money to fund their activities. There is no longer an expectation among top university managers that they simply deliver a traditional product with whatever money government provides. They feel they have to be entrepreneurial, treat students more like customers, and at the same time maintain their academic credibility. Third, quality standards may become an issue for a public sector organisation simply because of the work of audit bodies established by government. For whatever reason, there is now a high level of quality consciousness in public sector organisations, and many statements have been made about maintaining or even improving quality while delivering value for money.

The public may have also forced quality issues on to the agenda. The public has certainly elected governments and politicians who have sought higher quality in the delivery of public services. But the interactions between service users and providers at the service delivery interface have been more challenging in recent years. Service users are more likely to question the quality of the services provided and to challenge decisions made by public services officials. The rise in consumerism among public service users has been a gradual one and public services organisations have responded to it or encouraged it in a number of ways, from improving complaint procedures through to using market research methods such as focus groups. Students at universities, for example, are becoming slightly more likely than in the past to act as active consumers: they prefer programmes with more options and flexibility, they are critical of poor teaching, and they may turn to legal processes to challenge decisions of the universities.

The quality of public service is increasingly judged in terms of accessibility. In the past it seemed as though public service providers only looked at service delivery from a provider point of view. A commonly experienced example is provided by the hospital out-patients' clinic. Patients could spend hours waiting to be seen by the doctor. It was as if the doctor's time was precious but the patient's time did not matter at all. Accessing this particular service required a great deal of patience by patients. Public service managers are being expected to take more responsibility for the consumer experience of accessing and using a service. This new expectation creates issues for public service organisations. For example, some public services cover areas that are both urban and rural and the service users may find more difficulty in getting information about services and then getting access to the services themselves. Of course, we should not exaggerate the contrast with past practices. Library services, for example, have often found ways of providing access to their services for people who found it difficult to travel to libraries. Access issues are not only a product of the physical distance between users and service outlets. Service provider behaviour and capability often produce them. Many people living in urban centres have found a lack of information and advice a great barrier to accessing services. They have encountered petty bureaucratic officials who were unable or reluctant to divulge information or provide help. They have also found it difficult to get help with problems that require that they contact a range of public service agencies, each providing only a part of the solution. In this case, the access problem was aggravated by providers being organised on a basis that made sense to them but did not make much sense to the members of the public.

A final meaning of accessibility is linked to social inclusion. Some public services have provided disproportionate benefits to some segments of the population and done much less for others. This can show up in the life chances of people and unequal opportunities for access to a high quality of life. Universities, for example, mainly served the upper and middle social classes in the first half of the twentieth century. This influenced not only what they taught but also how they taught it. This history has constructed a particular view of the quality standards of a university education. This is being challenged, and access to higher education is being widened. This had led to some questioning of the meaning of quality higher education. This has not yet been finally resolved, and so the definition of quality standards has been controversial for a number of years. However, in Britain, governmental policy and resource decisions are creating new pressures on universities in terms of how they ensure they are delivering a high-quality service to the public.

Restructuring has been a common and thorny issue in many organisations. In some cases this has been triggered by budgetary difficulties. Chief executives have had to restructure staffing and operational activities. The aims have been to realign service delivery with new realities of budgeting, but in a way that did not harm the benefits being offered to service users. Where restructuring has been successful, service innovations and new attitudes among staff have created more confidence and optimism among those who work in public service organisations. The price has been periods of conflict and uncertainty, as customary ways of working and operating rules were renegotiated.

ISSUE MANAGEMENT IN PRACTICE

How are public sector managers handling or responding to these issues? There are three generic strategies for handling or managing issues:

1. Actions to deal with resource constraints.
2. Actions to target community needs better.
3. Actions to improve organisational performance.

Actions to deal with resource constraints

In the last couple of decades more public sector managers have been giving up the idea that their organisations should pursue their mandates largely on the basis of self-sufficiency. In many cases public sector organisations have a long history of outsourcing and working in partnership. But these were seen as marginal and unimportant mechanisms, whereas now managers are expected to give full consideration to the benefits of these options.

Experience of outsourcing has often been a positive one in relation to service delivery functions, even when it has been done on a compulsory basis. Putting work out to tender has produced many instances of services that have been improved through streamlining, better management, and increased investment.

Working in alliances with other organisations has grown in importance both for tackling community problems as well as for service delivery. There has been, for example, the creation of networks of organisations to provide support systems for people with mental health problems, people with learning difficulties, and elderly people. In the latter case, government organisations have developed geriatric services in the community as an alternative to placing elderly people in hospital to receive support and treatment. This has meant bringing together social services, health services, and voluntary sector organisations. The motivation for such alliances and networks is in part the aspiration to create a better quality of life for the people concerned. There is also an aim, in some cases, to make public money go further. Hospital care, for example, is expensive, and if support networks can help people earlier on then it may be possible to reduce the use of hospitals.

Partnerships in the regulatory area seem to offer an alternative to expensive and probably unacceptable levels of regulation by getting partner organisations to comply voluntarily with socially desirable practices and standards. Partnerships may focus on major community problems, such as those associated with the environment, and may achieve results and an alleviation of problems not easily achieved by traditional methods of government. Local authorities, for example, have prompted partner organisations to promote recycling, conservation, and sustainable use of natural resources.

Partnership working is increasingly found taking place between government organisations. Serious community problems often straddle geographical boundaries and some adjacent local government organisations have begun to work together on them. By combining their resources two local authorities may achieve more impact on community problems of economic regeneration. The pressure on their budgets and services make such collaboration more appealing. Regeneration projects mounted by two authorities working together can be larger and have a more noticeable impact than smaller projects run by a single local authority.

Partnership working assumes its most ambitious form in the idea and practice of community governance and leadership. Local government organisations hope to develop working relationships with other organisations that will be instrumental in realising a higher quality of life for people living in a city, town, or local area. Instead of attempting to construct this higher quality of life through a tax and spend approach to government, they seek to mobilise and align the resources of these partner organisations behind a strategic vision for the community. By catalysing resources of others, they aim to go beyond the current limitations of their own direct financial power (Osborne & Gaebler 1992).

The quality of life of people in a community is increasingly seen as a function of community partners working together on problem solving rather than simple service delivery. The problems of a community, which can cut across the mandates of individual departments and public agencies, include issues such as drug problems, crime and disorder, youth issues, social exclusion, unemployment, and environmental issues. The terms for working together may be based on a written strategy, but this is a document that is useful to the extent that the partners have correctly defined the exact nature of the problem and found solutions that will work. For example, local governments work with the police and others to improve community safety. The problem of community safety cannot be totally understood in terms of official crime statistics. The partners will need to research the public's experiences and priorities (using focus groups, large-scale surveys, and community forums). This research may well lead the partners to question their own initial understanding of the problems and to formulate the actual problems in ways that require new forms of intervention and action.

Resource constraints may require changes in activities by public sector organisations. Retrenchment by cutting back on activities across the board is not feasible where the resource constraints apply year after year, and where politicians place pressure on public sector managers to achieve improved results with smaller budgets. Cuts may be sought by reducing management costs while protecting front-line services. All areas of activity may be scrutinised, with senior managers looking at what units do and the resources they use. Unit managers may be asked how they can do what they do more cheaply. Asking whether something has to be done or really needs to be done may cut frills in service delivery. Such detailed scrutiny may discover substantial savings with minimal reductions in the value of the activities in the eyes of the public. Ideally, the public sector organisation responds to resource constraints not merely by well-directed cuts but also by being innovative and creative. This, however, is far from automatic. There have to be the right political and cultural conditions, as well as skilled and motivated champions of change, for pressure on budgets to produce innovation.

Actions to target community needs better

Public sector organisations have often relied on legislation and professional advice to define the needs of the public. In recent years top managers in the public services are saying that they also need the views of the public in order to design services properly. This involves seeing things through the eyes of the public. To return to the example of community safety, top public sector managers are insisting that they require knowledge of what the public feels. An effective police service is not simply one that brings about a fall in crime statistics. It is effective if people begin to feel safer living in their communities. Moreover, there is a need to understand the factors that are important in people feeling safe. Such understanding may lead to different measures from the obvious one of employing more police officers to catch and charge those responsible for crime and disorder.

The role of local government in targeting community needs better is a distinctive one. As local government takes up this role it inevitably has to rethink what community needs matter most and how it should be involved in meeting those needs. It is questioning its traditional service delivery role. In the UK, local government has owned and managed public housing, run schools, provided social services, delivered library and leisure services, as well as carried out a range of regulatory functions through inspections and enforcement. As community leaders, local authorities take a lead on identifying what a community's needs are and working with partner organisations to address those needs. This is a very different role. In place of the power to provide and run services for the public, the public sector organisation seeks influence on behalf of the community to meet the top priority needs. This should be seen as a growing scope for the pursuit of public interests, even though the budgetary resources remain limited. All things being equal, the growth of community leadership activities by public sector leaders should identify a critical local dimension to the needs being identified. The overall themes may be the same—economic regeneration, environmental problems, drugs, community safety, and so on, but the locality will give these a specific content. So, in one community the regeneration needs may be centred on the development of a better infrastructure for a key local industry. In another community, regeneration may need to concentrate on widening the business base and encouraging more small business. In one community, there may be localised pockets of deprivation, unemployment, and poor housing. In another area there may be particular environmental pollution problems. The needs of an inner-city community will be very different from those of a leafy suburban area. And the needs of both of these could be very different from those of a rural community.

In tackling the issues thrown up by a community leadership role, public sector leaders are increasingly redefining their role away from service delivery. But it is not merely through partnership working with other public agencies and other organisations that community needs will be identified and addressed. Senior managers in public sector organisations have often accepted the existence of a long-run decline of communities based on kinship and neighbourhoods. High levels of crime, poor educational levels, and high unemployment in inner-city areas may be considered to have

compounded the problems of transient and fragmented populations. In the face of this, public sector leaders may advocate a role
for their organisations in community development. Quite modest
sums of money may be used to employ people to work on community development. If this community development work is infused
with an agenda for community empowerment, the community development specialists may lay considerable emphasis on learning
by the community. Part of this work is supporting the community
in its efforts to learn about and articulate its own needs. Part of the
work is supporting the community in identifying and creating its
own resources to address its needs. This can be justified as the
public sector helping neighbourhoods to work better. In such
neighbourhoods people help themselves and form more active and
resourceful communities. So, public sector leaders aspire to mobilise communities in order that the people in the community can act
on their own needs.

Actions to improve organisational performance

Public sector managers can use a range of measures to improve
organisational performance. There is obviously action to improve
the organisation by paying more attention to the motivation of
employees. This can be expected to have a general beneficial effect
on performance, helping to achieve higher levels of productivity and
quality.

A second type of measure is to improve leadership performance.
Leadership is responsible for providing direction and control. This
is especially important for a public sector organisation that is striving to achieve a very ambitious strategic vision. To improve
organisational performance the leadership must set challenging
targets (but not so challenging that management becomes overextended and key activities become critically impaired). These
targets may be related to the strategic vision and financial resources within a strategic plan. Leadership is then needed to align
and co-ordinate activities of departments and units so as to
implement the strategic plan. If successful, the leadership will get a
contribution to improved organisational performance by better
co-ordination and a more corporate approach within departments
and units. This is particularly important where the issues being

managed are community issues that by their very nature seem to require a response from across the organisation (as well as across public agencies). Leadership efforts may need to be directed towards making professional specialists, departments, and units see the interrelated nature of activities and the benefits of co-operation to tackle the issues. The ability of the leadership to do this is enhanced by the existence of an effective executive team. The members of the executive, working with the chief executive to provide the managerial leadership of the public sector organisation, need themselves to be able to appreciate the benefits of a corporate approach to issue management.

Assuming that measures to motivate employees and provide effective leadership have been used, the final option for building organisational performance in relation to issue management is action to invest in and develop capability. Some investment may be needed in buildings. The buildings used by a public sector organisation can have a big impact on its ability to handle resource and service delivery issues. It may be important to invest in buildings and facilities not only to enable higher efficiency, but also to provide better working conditions for staff. More and more senior public sector managers are looking to investments in information technology to help with tackling issues of efficiency in service delivery and improved communication with the public. Finally, public sector organisations are looking for ways to develop and share skills, and are seeking to develop skills through measures which are in keeping with ideas of the 'learning organisation'. In the increasingly dynamic environment of the public sector, this means cross-department learning and skill sharing.

SUMMARY AND CONCLUSIONS

Over the last decade the strategic issues facing public sector managers and how they are managed have been evolving. The main rationale for paying attention to issues from a management point of view is that this is the way to build an effective leadership that is capable of setting a strategic direction and implementing strategic change. From the public's point of view, issue management is needed alongside management of service delivery to maintain the relevance and value of public sector management. The issues are numerous and various, but can be summarised as resource issues, needs issues, and organisational issues. The key measures that are being used to address these issues include: outsourcing, partnership working, community development, researching the needs of the public, community leadership, and organisational development (motivation of employees, leadership, and investing and developing facilities, technology, and resources).

5
Vision

We start this chapter with a general understanding that public sector organisations exist to meet social or public needs. The strategic leadership of a public sector organisation will have to take cognisance of the objectives of elected politicians in setting their goals. It may be assumed that these objectives, as a result of democratic processes, represent a legitimate statement of the social needs to be served. These objectives, however, are often framed so broadly, and with little awareness of operational contingencies, that chief executives and others share in the responsibility of defining organisational goals which meet social needs. By necessity, the goals will be related to some degree to the agenda of the elected politicians to whom the chief executive is ultimately or even directly accountable. But the chief executive will shape the goals to take account of other operational contingencies as well. For instance, goals will need to be achievable in terms of organisational capacities and values, both those that exist actually, and those that might be developed through strategic action (Heymann 1987). Chief executives will also shape the goals and the plans to realise them. They will take into account the need to obtain or maintain political support, public support, and to form and maintain alliances and co-operative relations with other organisations that impact on the organisation's ability to accomplish its goals.

Top managers in the public sector very often consider it important that their organisation expresses its goals in the form of a strategic vision. Top managers often see constructing and disseminating the vision statement as a clear leadership responsibility. Indeed, chief executives may feel a personal responsibility for ensuring that their organisation is equipped with a vision statement.

A vision may be defined as an ideal future state. Beckhard & Harris (1987, p. 45) report that: 'Today more and more attention is being paid, in both the planning process and determination of managerial strategies, to articulating the "vision", or desired end state, of the leaders and managers of the change.' Visions can be phrased in a concrete way and consist of descriptions of new activities or new services. Sometimes these may be expressed in a very pithy and all-encompassing way. In this book, visions are not assumed to be statements of corporate values.

If there is to be a vision then there should be some idea when this vision will be achieved. Many top public sector managers find long-term changes very difficult to think about. Writing about strategic planning in the public sector, Wilkinson & Monkhouse (1994, p. 17) claim that: 'The distance chosen for the time horizon is not critical and current experience suggests that three to five years is as far as is realistic in the current climate of change.' In contrast, Bushnell & Halus (1992, p. 360) suggest that a 'minimum time frame might be five years' but 'could be as long as forty years, as dictated by the realities of a given program'. In fact, there is no systematic evidence to demonstrate that the distance chosen for the time horizon is not critical. Strategic vision may need to be far-sighted. A public sector organisation may need to look 10 or 20 years into the future and provide a target for the future state of the organisation. A hospital might say that by the year 2020 it wants to achieve world-class status in a number of medical specialities.

The definition of a vision could be positioned early in the chain of strategic management steps, before strategic issues and actions have been planned, and especially before the work of planning budgets and activities to focus and align the organisation with the strategic direction (Nutt & Backoff 1992). However, it may be seen as coming towards the end of the analytical steps in strategic planning (Wilkinson & Monkhouse 1994; Bryson 1995).

In perhaps the simplest model imaginable of strategic management in the public sector, the top managers (possibly working with elected politicians) draw up a strategic vision that is a desired future state and compare that vision with the current state of the organisation (its activities, structures, and results). Then they draw up a strategic plan to move the organisation to the future desired state, perhaps taking account of barriers to change.

In this chapter we will look at the different functions of a strategic vision, what is contained in a strategic vision, and how they are produced.

THE FUNCTIONS OF A STRATEGIC VISION

A strategic vision may be seen as useful for obtaining a consensus on the organisation's goals. Public sector managers may be particularly interested in seeing this consensus cover all levels of management, politicians, and employees. They need the support of politicians. Managers may see a strategic vision statement as useful as a mechanism for building the support of politicians. This requires that the politicians are convinced that their political priorities are reflected in the vision statement, and that this vision statement will make a difference to the effectiveness of the organisation.

The managers need employees to understand and feel committed to the organisation's goals. A new chief executive will assess the extent to which people employed by the organisation have an understanding of what is being required of them. If this understanding is absent, then the new chief executive may diagnose the need for work on a strategic vision statement.

A vision statement may be valued for the impact on team spirit throughout the organisation. Obviously this requires a vision statement that has some impact in terms of inspiring people, and the organisation needs to have the ability to communicate the statement and convey the credibility of the strategic intent. Nevertheless, the use of a strategic vision to create a collaborative organisational community has obvious appeal.

A new chief executive also looks to see how well an organisation's capabilities, activities, and resources are aligned with its goals. If there are serious deficiencies in capacity and misalignments of activities and resources, the new chief executive may well diagnose the need to establish or strengthen the organisation's use of strategic management processes. He or she may start by establishing a clear statement of the strategic vision and then proceed to make a plan for strategic changes.

The development of a strategic vision statement by top management may also serve to foster a more corporate approach within the organisation. This is particularly important in the context of public organisations involved in new community planning initiatives. In local government, for example, where multi-purpose structures sometimes lead to a strong emphasis on departmental or professional goals, the arrival of a corporate approach means a shift to 'joined up' government. This necessitates thinking holistically about the interrelationships of community issues and the overlapping of departmental mandates. Strategic visions can provide an impetus to more corporate mindedness by stressing themes that emerge as issues from community planning.

The strategic vision statement, if it is effectively communicated and monitored, can create dilemmas and ambiguities for managers who are mainly pursuing their traditional functional responsibilities. Senior managers have an important role to play in getting these managers to place their functional responsibilities within the framework provided by the strategic goals set by corporate levels of management. Therefore, this is about getting departments to play their part in terms of the whole organisation. If community safety is a theme of the strategic vision, then senior management may look for a contribution to the achievement of corporate targets from home care services, education departments, youth services, and many others. If social exclusion is the theme, then housing services may have a key role to play in supporting tenancies of client groups that are easily and frequently excluded from community participation.

To the extent that strategic visions are used to bring about comprehensive strategic change and increase the value of public services, the strategic vision is useful in shifting the balance away from provider interests to service user interests. The public sector is increasingly taking the view that while the public service employee is valued, the public sector has got to be restructured to serve the public better. This is seen as a major turning point in the development of the public sector, and strategic visions and mission statements are seen as a tool of reconstruction. The mission statement provides an important basis for the accountability mechanisms that will be used to ensure that the public sector produces results for the public. The vision statement plays more of a role in designing the strategic changes that produce the benefits for service users in the long term.

Vision statements are also useful in developing partnership working. Top managers in the public sector spend significant amounts of time in partnership working with other public, private, and voluntary organisations. This working, to be fruitful, involves building a shared strategic agenda. This provides a context for the negotiations and agreements about the costs and benefits of partnerships, and the elaboration of a strategic vision is part of the persuasion and convincing that accompanies the negotiations between partners.

DEFINITION OF A STRATEGIC VISION

A strategic vision is an articulation of what a public sector organisation should be doing in the long term and what it is trying to achieve. This might be expressed more formally as a far-sighted statement of an organisation's strategic goals in terms of what new activities the organisation should undertake in the future and what new benefits will result for the public. A university might say something about what type of educational market it should be in. It might say something about the educational services it should be offering and the kinds of benefits it should offer its stakeholders. This may be based on research and analysis of environmental trends. It may be based on an audit of current strengths and weaknesses of the university. The analysis of the environment and strengths and weaknesses leads to the statement of what the university should be doing in the future, and the vision statement should then provide a clear idea about how the university will need to be reshaped as it moves into the future.

The vision statement may help with the identification of the developmental challenges of a public sector organisation. In the case of a university, the vision statement may help with the identification of the skills that will be required by university staff. If, for example, the university intends that it will be a major player in educating international students, or it intends that regional employers will think naturally of turning to the university with consultancy assignments, then it will need to recruit, train, and develop staff with the requisite skills.

It may be useful to distinguish between a 'genuine' strategic vision that is used by a public sector organisation to launch an ambitious strategic change programme, and a strategic vision statement that is prepared because organisations feel obliged to have one. In the latter case, the strategic vision statement may include ideas that have become widely endorsed, but the statement may lack credibility as a document that will provide a reference point for innovation and strategic experiments.

A genuine strategic vision provides a guiding system to drive strategic change programmes. These programmes are needed to change operating systems and create value for the public. Indeed, without strategic visions changes to operating processes must be arbitrary or spontaneous. The vision may be useful in a technical way because it indicates what changes to make in operating processes and the path to take in creating new value for the public. Perhaps most usefully, strategic visions can express a view about what service users of the future will value.

Strategic visions also have a social importance in providing a rationale for change. Top managers need good strategic visions for the purpose of achieving consent as much as for the quality of the ideas contained in them. Therefore, strategic visions need to be framed in a way that makes them useful for purposes of communication and debate, and they need top managers who know how to communicate them and debate them to convince employees and others that they make good sense. It is an obvious point, but worth underlining: change works better when people have been persuaded that the change is for a worthwhile purpose.

Genuine strategic visions are also an asset for discussions with other organisations about forming consortiums to work in partnership to improve public services and make better use of public resources. The strategic vision of where an organisation wants to go in the future can be a useful framework for discussing collaboration. The public sector organisation may persuade other organisations that this is a worthwhile future for the consortium partners to pursue jointly. Conversely, there may be a need to discuss how the separate strategic visions can be realigned for mutual benefit.

Discussions of strategic visions by organisations forming a consortium provide a way of employing a win–win model to frame the terms of the collaboration. Providing there is a platform of openness and trust, all partners can discuss how benefits for all the partners can be obtained from realignments of strategic visions. This shifts the emphasis from a traditional public sector insularity that led to defensiveness and turf wars. Indeed, the presentation and discussion of strategic visions can provide an agenda to work on during which trust and understanding can be increased.

To the extent that a strategic vision is a set of ideas about the future, there is obviously a question about just how many years ahead must a manager look for it to be a strategic vision rather than a short-term aim. Many public managers think they should be planning long term, but feel that this is difficult to do in the light of political processes that pressurise them for results in the short term. Others have problems with the concept of a strategic vision because of the difficulties of making predictions. How will Europe develop? What will be the impact of information technology on the public sector? How will trends in health, employment, the world of work, etc. develop over the next 20 years? How will lifestyle trends impact on the demand for public services? However, in the face of all these uncertainties, most public managers feel that decision making is too short term.

Some sense can be rescued for the idea of a strategic vision from the chaos and uncertainties of environmental trends. This is the sense that strategic vision is an ambition rather than a simple prediction. The chief executive of the public sector organisation knows that the strategic vision is what they would like to happen. It is a target to work towards; it is not a predicted destination. A local authority may have an ambition to be a great place to live and work. A hospital may have an ambition to be a centre of medical excellence—at least in national terms. A university may have an ambition to produce the most capable and employable graduates. These are ambitions to be pursued. They are ambitions that become increasingly integrated into the identity of the organisation, and then start to weave themselves into the culture of the organisation. But only if that ambition is real and can be expressed in strategic changes that testify to the seriousness and commitment of the organisation to the ambition. As time goes on, the organisation measures everything that it does against this ambition, and everyone knows how the top managers are likely to react to any events, because they know that they are dedicated to achieving this ambition.

Having a strong strategic vision does not mean that there is no opportunism in the decisions of top managers. They have to have regard to developments in the environment that can threaten or assist strategic change. It does not mean that the organisation is at all times making progress towards the strategic vision. There are times when retreats are forced on top managers even when there is a strong strategic vision.

But however much opportunism there is, and however many retreats are forced, the essence of the strategic vision in the public sector is focusing on the benefits for the public in general, for service users, and for future generations of service users.

THE MAIN ELEMENTS OF MODERN STRATEGIC VISIONS

The strategic visions of public sector organisations involved in big change programmes tend to have a number of common elements.

The first element is an emphasis on enabling and problem solving. Consequently, strategies may have an outward focus and are not merely blueprints for developing service delivery processes. This aspect of a strategic vision implies a long-term and comprehensive transition for any public sector organisation. It is in part a matter of fostering a mixed economy in service delivery. It is in part about empowering service users, who may want to design services that take advantage of opportunities for service user management. For example, a traditional model of public sector leisure services would involve the public sector bearing the capital and revenue costs of leisure centres built to serve residential communities. It is possible to use planning powers to get development companies to bear the capital costs, and representatives of the community to manage leisure facilities. Moreover, it has been possible for statutory agencies to influence the design of these facilities to include activities that maximise opening hours and income so that revenue costs are covered by charges.

Such a strategic vision of the future of public services necessitates that top managers in the public sector develop much more of an external role. It requires the development of new and adaptable skills, and much less reliance on traditional bureaucratic skills. It requires managers who focus on activities that produce good outcomes for the public rather than the application of traditional service and professional skills.

This leads to a second common feature of the strategic visions of modern public sector organisations. This is a strong strategic intent to be responsive to service users. This may be contrasted with the bureaucratic ethos of many public sector organisations in the past. In thinking about service users, the strategic visions are likely to express a commitment to new 'functionalities' in the services that will be increasingly offered. An example from higher education may illustrate this point. The traditional university professional acts on the basis that undergraduates need to be educated by providing them with knowledge. The student is regarded as needing to be filled up with the accumulated wisdom to be found in scholarly books and academic journal articles. The library and the lecture room are the essential learning environments for the traditional university system. A modern university, embarking on a major programme of change to deliver an entirely new kind of higher education, is likely to take the view that this is only a part of what the student experience should involve. A modern university articulates a strategic vision for how resources, staff, equipment, buildings, and students can be developed into a potent learning environment. It reconceptualises its mission as one of placing the student experience at the centre of the educational process. The functionality is conceived in terms of learning outcomes—what students are able to do at the end of their education—not what they know. So, the strategic vision of modern public sector organisations not only expresses a deep commitment to responsiveness to the needs of service users, it also reconceptualises the nature of the benefit which is the intended outcome of public service delivery.

A third common element of current strategic visions in the public sector is the intention to make use of partnerships or alliances in a variety of ways. While partnership working can remain at the margins of public sector activities early in the strategic transition, there can be no doubt that strategic visions are making increasingly bold claims for the need for partnerships. This reflects the challenging nature of the community issues the public sector is facing. As we have noted above, the public sector is being expected to deal with complex and difficult issues: environmental, economic regeneration, crime and disorder, youth issues, social exclusion, etc. The leaders of public sector organisations are saying through their foresights about the future of their organisations that there will be less emphasis on delivering direct services and more emphasis on working in partnership with other organisations. The formation of coalitions or consortiums composed of local authorities, voluntary groups, health authorities, private sector businesses, and community groups is commonplace. However, some partnerships are weaker than others because of limited experience and sometimes wariness about some forms of cross-boundary working. Partnerships with the private sector may be harder to form and maintain than those with, say, the voluntary sector. There are bound to be issues of agreeing how risks will be shared between public and private sector partners. Successful partnerships will make demands on the current core competencies of public sector organisations. They will have to learn how to develop, combine, and leverage skills and techniques that are important for making and using alliance relationships.

Strategic visions attuned to partnership working are bound to differ in important ways from a previous era in which strategic vision was hitched mainly to organisational achievements. Inasmuch as the strategic vision is important in the dialogue between partners, then it must contain themes and issues that might easily form a shared issue agenda for the partners. So, we might find, for example, the theme of social exclusion as a priority for collective action, and thus appearing on the strategic issue agenda of a consortium. This would imply that social exclusion becomes a theme in the strategic vision of a number of separate organisations—including private sector businesses.

In practice, national and federal governments are playing an increasingly important role in defining these themes. They promote them and encourage public sector agencies to pick them up. They stress the need for joint action on these themes through exhortation (the idea of 'joined up' government) and through vetting strategic plans of public sector organisations.

There is much about modern strategic visions that concerns or implies innovation. However, performance and results are given strong emphasis in these strategic visions. The idea of 'doing more with less' has become a hackneyed phrase, but the political pressure to keep public spending down is virtually universal. At this turning point in the development of public sector management, the inclusion of efficiency and performance in the strategic vision may be seen as applicable to the direct service delivery role of public sector organisations. The connection with partnership working and catalysing community problem solving is still very often ambiguous in the vision of chief executives and other top managers. The application of performance management and strategic planning for performance may be seen as mainly concerned with service delivery. Logically, however, there is a case for seeing partnership working and regulatory activities as covered by the performance management discipline that stresses the use of public money to achieve the best value possible for the public.

Finally, strategic visions in modern public sector organisations often stress an end to the petty secrecy and inflexibility practised by older bureaucratic forms of public services. This is symptomatic of the transformational nature of the change programmes being launched by public sector organisations. This transformation entails building a new relationship with the public. This is a relationship to be built on the empowerment of the public. This requires, at the very least, openness and responsiveness. These are the two primary values that are being enshrined in new habits of public sector management. They are essential if the public sector is going to acquire an ability to deliver the new functionalities that public services need to meet the requirements of the public as service users. Without openness and responsiveness the activities of the public sector remain fixed in old paternalistic patterns of operation.

FORMING THE IDEAS FOR STRATEGIC VISION STATEMENTS

A strategic vision or point of view has to be produced. Organisations do not have them automatically or spontaneously. It is evident that individual public sector organisations when writing vision statements are influenced by the strategic visions of other public sector organisations. There is, in other words, an element of imitation in drawing up vision statements.

Governments also promote themes and agendas, and these influence individual public sector organisations. Chief executives will draw up vision statements and strategic plans that consciously pick up national government themes and agendas. This is one way in which public sector reforms and modernisation are disseminated throughout large parts of the public sector. Consequently, if the national government is encouraging action on community safety, environmental issues, youth, old people, etc. then they become part of the vision and strategic goals of organisations in health, education, local government, and so on.

Some organisations are led by elected politicians. In their cases, the top managers can work with elected politicians on the statement of a strategic vision. The politicians have their political visions. A chief executive may even define his or her responsibility as working with elected politicians to develop a strategic vision for the organisation based on the politicians' political vision. In this case they may define their role as chief executive as to facilitate this process and then take primary responsibility for implementing the strategic vision.

A further way in which a vision statement can be produced is by community planning. Elected politicians and top managers from public sector organisations take part in community planning processes involving representatives of business, voluntary, and community organisations. The interactions and debates within community planning forums can help public sector managers develop greater empathy for current and future public needs. Out of this empathy may come ideas for worthwhile strategic visions for public sector organisations.

Chief executives may work with their boards and their top executive teams to form the ideas that make up the strategic vision. Some chief executives insist that it is the responsibility of the chief executive and top management to have strategic ideas. They define this as being an integral part of their responsibility for leading their organisations. This may be found, for example, in universities and health service organisations. This may be a far from easy process. Progress in forming the ideas may be painfully slow. Getting people to define their ideas, ensuring that these ideas are understood, and then bringing the ideas together to construct a picture of what the organisation should be doing and how it will be meeting the needs of the public is far from easy. This process needs to continue until the picture of the future is clear enough that those involved are able to draw out a series of strategic goals.

One issue that is little discussed arises when a chief executive works with his or her executive team on the vision statement (or strategic plan). This is the issue of the chief executive making sense of conflicting advice.

Research by Kakabadse et al. (1996) on leadership in the public found that some 56 per cent of a sample of 800 top civil servants from a European country believed that members of the senior management team held different views on the future direction of the organisation. This was much higher than for a sample of senior managers from National Health Service (NHS) Trust organisations in the UK. In the latter case only 20 per cent of top managers thought there were different views in the senior management team. Whatever the proportion, however, some differences of opinion among top management teams on strategic direction are bound to exist in many public sector organisations.

If the executive team tends to work by offering advice to the chief executive and then he or she makes the decision, there will be occasions when the advice conflicts. This may be easiest to deal with when two members of the executive team disagree. The chief executive has to make a choice between the advice offered. It will be harder when the executive team members all agree, but the chief executive disagrees with them. Chief executives in the last situation need to be good at judging when to defer to the advice and when to insist on their own right to make the decision. Ignoring the advice of an executive team should not be done lightly. The members are presumably experienced managers who are paid for their ability to make judgements, and so a chief executive is wise to listen to their ideas. In the end, of course, chief executives are the ones who should be held mainly responsible and this justifies their prerogative to back their own judgement on occasion.

The final ingredient for forming vision statements, unless you believe in vision statements as purely intuitive products of visionary leaders, is good information on what is happening. This information relates to what is happening to the communities and service users that are served by the public sector organisation. This may involve collecting information on trends, or on events that are expected to impact on the community or the service users. Above all else, for a public sector organisation, is the need for good quality information on what is happening to lifestyles and thus the needs of groups of people living in the community. Information is used mainly to prepare for thinking about vision statements. The chief executives and senior managers who write vision statements like to have a 'feel' for what is going on. The information is not subjected to sophisticated or obscure technical processes to produce a vision statement. Well-informed senior managers with a good feel for what is happening and for what the impacts of various events may be, draw on this information to support their forecasts of what the organisation should be doing.

It would be wrong to assume that the most important information for vision statements arrives on the desks of top managers in the form of information briefs and quantitative data. Increasingly, as partnership working has become more widespread in the public sector, information about trends, events, and discontinuities becomes known at many different points in any single public sector organisation. A chief executive and a management team that wishes to make use of this information thus needs to have a good idea of where knowledge is lodged within the organisation. For example, a university may need information on employment, regional problems, and what happens to students after they have left the university. This information may be accessed by talking to careers service staff, staff in alumni units, research groups, and particular individuals across the university.

WORKING WITH POLITICIANS ON VISION STATEMENTS

In cases where public sector managers have direct contact with elected politicians (as in local government) then managers may be more likely to say that their role is not to formulate strategic direction. They may say that their role is about making sure that the politicians' strategic direction is implemented. They may seek to influence and advise on the strategic direction, but they will feel more comfortable about taking responsibility for finding the paths through which strategic intentions can be realised than about proposing vision statements.

Much depends on the character and extent of the ambitions of the politicians. If politicians have strong ambitions for public service, then it is more likely that they will want to lay down a strategic vision and set a strategic direction for managers to implement. These ambitions may centre on the quality of life experienced by citizens and the rate of progress in improving the quality of life.

Managers can help politicians to articulate the ambitions and vision statements that define the strategic direction to be taken by the organisation. One way of doing this is by setting up strategy retreats or workshops in which politicians are helped to think about what the organisation should be doing in, say, 10 years' time. Such occasions may rely heavily on brainstorming techniques, but they need also to tackle uncomfortable issues and examine deeply held assumptions. In other words, there should be some degree of challenge in the process. This assumes that there are basic assumptions that constrain the visioning of the future and that they need also to be put under the spotlight if the quality of strategic visioning is to be high. For example, politicians holding traditional welfare state assumptions may find it uncomfortable to consider a future in which service delivery is less important, and public sector organisations design their activities on principles of service user empowerment and partnership working. There may be other assumptions based on past achievements that are more specific to particular organisations. Politicians may take pride in forms of organisation or public facilities that are no longer optimum for emerging lifestyles. This may be based on past struggles to establish policies and find funding for projects. But as communities move on, politicians need to revise their assumptions about the nature of public services. Again, strategy retreats and workshops need to enter into uncomfortable debates that are about questioning the continued relevance of such assumptions.

Not all elected politicians want a role in strategy processes or wish to take part in strategy retreats or workshops. Traditional political attitudes may cause some politicians to look with suspicion on management techniques in general. But it is not just a matter of suspicion based on political dogma. Some politicians see in the special language of strategic management a ploy by managers to avoid getting on with the main work of implementing the decisions of politicians. Some politicians may see strategic management processes as a waste of time—a bit of self-indulgence and self-justification engaged in by professional managers. They may find the talk of vision statements just unnecessary management-speak.

Chief executives and senior managers may have to work hard to persuade reluctant politicians to take part in strategy retreats and workshops. They may have to work hard to convince them that the process is a useful exercise and important for the long-term effectiveness of the organisation. The politicians may feel that the managers should be concentrating on sorting out poor quality services and fixing activities that are causing complaints by the public— that is, sorting out the basics of operations. If the managers want a vision statement from the politicians they may find themselves explaining not only why the organisation and employees need vision statements, but also that the politicians themselves need a vision statement. The top managers may point to the way in which vision statements create the intellectual launch pad for strategic projects and programmes to take the organisation to a successful long-term future. They may point to the benefits for internal morale if they can communicate to the workforce an idea of where the politicians want the organisation to go in the future. Basically, the managers argue that the political agenda is best served by creating a strategic agenda based on a vision statement and strategic goals. The managers need political visions to be translated into managerial terms.

CONSULTING ON THE IDEAS

Consultation on the strategic vision statement may take place when it exists in draft form. The statement may be published in draft form as part of a draft strategic plan for the organisation. One of the simplest ways of consulting on it is simply to send it out to employees and external stakeholders for comments. Consulting the public on vision statements and strategic plans may be done through such a process. Some public sector organisations may send out thousands of copies of draft vision statements and strategic plans. Written comments can be reviewed and the draft statement and plan revised accordingly.

Such immediate and widespread distribution of drafts is not always considered a sensible idea. Senior managers have to make judgements about the likely impact of such an action. For example, some organisations may have been through recent strategic planning processes, and vision statements may have been produced that subsequently failed to work. There may be a credibility problem for the announcement of optimistic and bold vision statements. Morale and self-confidence among managers and employees may be low. In these circumstances, top management may decide that a more gradual process of strategic change is needed for a while and that this can be achieved by working towards a strategic vision quietly.

IMPLEMENTING VISION STATEMENTS

Strategic vision statements may be included in strategic or corporate planning documents. The form of such written statements may vary a great deal. They may consist of catchy one-line statements, obviously mostly useful to include on promotional material and for internal marketing of the strategic plan to employees. They may be statements stringing together currently fashionable phrases taken from national government agendas. At their best, vision statements focus the organisation on a long-term objective of serving the public in a particular way that makes sense of the future needs of the public and the future capabilities and resources of the organisation.

Simply writing down vision statements (and statements of strategic plans) is the start of the process. Chief executives worry about the use that is going to be made of statements—about whether any use is going to be made of them. Will they be noticed, let alone used? This ultimately depends on the calibre of the chief executive and top managers. It is their responsibility to make sure strategic vision statements and strategic plans are used. Actions have to be taken and resources mobilised to bring about the vision and ensure strategic goals are accomplished. They have to make sure, in other words, that strategy statements are meaningful. They have to make sure that they have meaning through shaping the future.

The process of making sure that the strategic vision statement is implemented is mainly pursued through a performance management system. This begins with management identifying corporate aims and strategic goals on the basis of the vision statement. To keep the process manageable and the organisation focused, the number of strategic goals needs to be quite limited—maybe not more than five to eight strategic goals. These goals may be set for implementation over a 5–10-year time period. Then the strategic goals have to be rendered intelligible as operational goals and performance targets. These may be set to cover one-year periods, and might be fixed in such a way that each year's operational goals take the organisation a step closer to achieving the strategic goals. At the simplest, the performance targets over successive years create a paced improvement in organisational performance. Assuming that each strategic goal is associated with two or three operational goals and that each of these have one or two key performance targets, a large public sector organisation might have in the region of 10–20 key performance targets.

Some top managers consider that implementation of vision statements also occurs through inspiring all levels of management and employees within the organisation. They may attempt to communicate this directly to groups of employees through talks and presentation. They may ask a communication unit to take charge of putting the vision statement across to employees through the production of colourful brochures, CD-ROM, and 'roadshows'. They can also use employee magazines or newspapers, as well as formal induction processes for new employees, to communicate and promote the strategic vision of the organisation. The effectiveness of the leadership in obtaining commitment to strategic visions should be systematically assessed. The mechanisms used to communicate the strategic vision are far from perfect. Employee magazines and newspapers, for example, may not be influential and may not even be widely read. Employees may find them boring because they lack human-interest stories. Employees may distrust them because they just put a management 'spin' on everything that happens and are not balanced in the way they report events.

There may need to be different versions of strategic vision statements and corporate strategic plans for communicating ideas and intentions to different audiences. Publications for public consumption, for example, may be quite different from documents supplied to higher bodies or agencies for purposes of accountability to politicians.

SUMMARY AND CONCLUSIONS

In this chapter we began by exploring the arguments for developing a strategic vision. The usefulness of a strategic vision for obtaining a consensus, developing a team feeling, overcoming departmentalism, moving away from provider mindsets, and forming partnerships was mentioned. The definition of a strategic vision was explored, and its main contemporary elements outlined. The use of vision and plans to formulate strategies in the public sector was considered. Ideas of public sector strategy were considered. This led to us to the idea of a vision statement as a far-sighted vision of what activities a public sector organisation will be involved in, who will benefit from its activities, and what organisations will be working in alliance with it or supporting it.

In the last part of this chapter we have looked at how ideas for a vision statement are formed, how managers may work with politicians on creating a vision statement, how consultation may be carried out, and how vision statements are implemented through performance management and communication processes.

6

Involving Managers and Employees

INTRODUCTION

It is often argued that the days of 'command and control' management systems are a thing of the past (Mellors 1996). More people-management skills are seen as essential for senior management. In this chapter we look more closely at the processes by which managers and employees can be involved in thinking about the future of the public sector organisation. This was looked at briefly in Chapter 5, but here we will examine the issues more deeply.

The chapter begins by outlining the reasons for involving managers and employees. Then we move on to consider what involving managers and employees exactly means. Finally, the various methods for involving managers and employees are described.

WHY INVOLVE MANAGERS AND EMPLOYEES?

Chief executives and top managers appear to spend a lot of time worrying about the amount of understanding of the need for strategic changes among managers and employees. Of course, they often mean by this not only comprehension but also commitment to change. They often believe that the problem of understanding is especially widespread in their kind of public sector organisation. This is a feature of public sector organisations that employ a large number of professionals. Thus, the chief executive may have decided on the strategic changes needed, and is concerned about the response he or she is getting from professional employees, who appear not to support the planned changes.

This appears to be the heart of what is labelled a communication problem. Experienced senior managers in the public sector expect to encounter this problem. They expect to have to expend a lot of effort communicating the need for change. This has been especially the case in the English health services, where the relationship between managers and professionals has been a tense and challenging one:

> Historically, hospitals have been seen as almost an ideal typical case of the professionalized organization (Bucher and Stelling 1977), characterised by shifting and organic professional segments largely autonomous of a marginal administration. The whole nature of health care systems came under challenge with the introduction of general management in the mid 1980s, with a strengthening of line management vis-à-vis the professionals (Pettigrew et al. 1992, pp. 9–10).

Managers are realistic about the chances of making a success of communicating with professional employees—they do not expect complete agreement and commitment. Nevertheless, even experienced public sector managers can become frustrated with the continual requirement to explain and convince employees. On occasion, in the face of professional scepticism, managers may wish they were in a greenfield site with a totally new set of staff who would throw themselves enthusiastically behind plans for change. They become frustrated with foot-dragging employees who claim not to know about the changes that have been planned. Communication is still seen as a central problem for public sector managers.

Involving managers and employees in thinking about the future of the organisation is one way of top management trying to get them to support strategic change. Consequently, thinking about the future is very often aimed at challenging existing activities to create support for activities that are envisioned in desired future states of the organisation. In a local authority this involves challenging service delivery activities and creating an acceptance for the need for more partnership activities and community problem solving. In the health service it involves challenging the pre-eminence of curative medicine and hospitals so that preventative activities and community health services can become more important. In the universities it involves challenging the importance placed on lectures and knowledge so that more space can be found for student-centred activities and the development and assessment of skills.

The assumption running through this argument is that chief executives and top managers in the public sectors are the main people who induce change, and that they have to find ways to take reluctant employees with them. In fact, this is not the whole story. The main sources of change in the public sector are the politicians. Chief executives and top managers occupy a key mediating role between politicians and people who work in the public sector. Consequently, it often looks as though it is the managers who are instigating change. Experienced public sector managers, especially when they have a lot of contact with elected politicians in the course of their work, know that managing change involves them in a brokering role. They broker changes between the politicians and the public on one hand, and the professionals and other employees on the other. In consequence of their mediating role and the brokering activities implied, chief executives in the public sector have an important influence in helping other employees to understand what is politically acceptable.

In some go-ahead organisations that have introduced teamworking, employees have been involved in thinking and planning ahead. It is important that this thinking and planning for the future by teams of employees is evaluated. Managers, who do this evaluation, inevitably have to do some channelling of this thinking. Not all ideas for the future can be pursued. In the case of the public sector, some of these ideas cannot be pursued because they are not consistent with legal mandates. Some cannot be pursued because they are not consistent with the policies and decisions of the elected politicians who have oversight of the public sector organisation. The managers who have contact with the elected politicians have to advise the teams that some of their proposals are not, in these ways, politically acceptable.

Involving managers and employees in thinking about the future, and the consequent consideration of what is politically acceptable, is obviously beneficial to top managers in the sense that more people in the organisation end up internalising the limits of political support. The more this happens the easier it is for the chief executive and top managers to carry out their mediating role between the politicians and the rest of managers and employees in the public sector organisation.

There is at least one more reason for involving managers and employees in thinking about the future. This is the reason that it can generate and release ideas within the organisation. Some of these ideas may be ones the top managers find useful. This motive for involvement is more likely to appeal to chief executives and top managers who see themselves as leaders who empower others. Public sector chief executives who have read management books on how to create excellent organisations may well feel encouraged to see themselves as leaders who can provide the kind of leadership to front-line employees that inspires experiments and a climate in which ideas 'bubble up'.

THE NATURE OF INVOLVEMENT

An organisation can involve managers and employees in a variety of ways prior to the formation of a strategic plan. They can be interviewed or surveyed regarding their opinions on the main strategic issues the organisation will face in the future. They can be involved in seminars, workshops, and large-scale events in order to involve them in thinking about trends, events, strengths, and weaknesses that will be pertinent over the next 5 or 10 years. In this way managers and employees can have inputs into the strategic planning process before decisions have been firmed up. Involvement may be thought of as a bottom-up mechanism.

Walsall Council in the UK during 1995 provides an example of involving employees prior to final decisions being made. David Winchurch, the chief executive appointed in 1991, was a strong believer in including the employees in thinking about, and bringing about, changes. Beedon & Winchurch (1995, p. 43) describe how a two-day meeting on the corporate plan involving 'hundreds of people, both employees and customers' was planned and executed 'to create a collective vision and ideas for change'. Five hundred employees volunteered to attend the meeting and a sample was selected to represent all council employees. Three hundred people attended the meeting including 50 customers. David Winchurch made a speech at the meeting. 'I heard that the speech I had given that morning had missed the mark somewhat, and found myself learning from the process . . . ' (Beedon & Winchurch 1995, p. 44).

In some cases involvement is partially or even largely top-down. Involving managers and employees in thinking about the future can be top management promoting as well as obtaining ideas. When other methods of communicating, such as employee newspapers or reports down the management line, fail to get messages across, top managers may turn to involvement initiatives. Managers and employees are invited to think about the future and come up with ideas, but the parameters of the exercise are set so as to place the thinking within the change agenda decided by top management.

Involvement processes can be designed to maximise the opportunities for top managers to engage managers and employees in debate. The involvement process is thus valued for the dialogue it fosters between levels of the organisation, rather than for the decisions or suggestions that are made in the process. In this dialogue, top managers may be seeking to explain the constraints on the organisation and convince managers and employees of the need for change.

The nature of the dialogue depends on the decision-making styles of the top managers. In Bloomsbury DHA in the late 1980s a number of clinicians that had an interest in strategy had become 'oppositional'. Apparently this was 'often over what was seen as a hectoring management style or narrower questions such as medical records, or the distribution of cuts . . . ' (Pettigrew et al. 1992, p. 95). The mood changed, however, as a result of the arrival of a new district general manager. 'Bryan Harrison, the new District General Manager . . . had developed an interactive style which stressed interpersonal communication, and which was used to encourage some of the younger "strategic" clinicians to come out of the woodwork and engage the strategic management process' (Pettigrew et al. 1992, p. 96). This case study showed that some but not all professionals are interested in strategy, and that an interactive style of management could encourage some professionals to become involved.

If managers believe that they have made the right decisions but now have to concentrate on getting the need for the decisions across to staff, then managers and employees may find their ideas and suggestions are listened to but not used. Such a style is more likely where top managers have identified staff as inevitably reluctant to change. Top managers then make decisions they feel the external situation requires, and feel that they have to ignore likely staff reactions because these are expected to be negative. In this case, top managers see the staff as an 'institutionalised opposition' whose views can be ignored prior to decisions. It is quite possible to see most staff this way and still feel that involvement exercises are needed and useful. But the exercise is then about trying to talk as many staff as possible around to accepting the decisions. The top managers feel justified in this stance because they fear that listening to staff would mean doing nothing, and they would have failed to deliver the results that the organisation has been mandated to achieve. In a sense, they are deaf to staff views in order to deliver results for which politicians hold them accountable.

Another variant on the involvement process, especially for involving operational managers in thinking about the future, is where top managers delegate the production of strategic plans. The chief executive or top management team may direct managers to prepare a strategic plan for their part of the organisation and to have it ready by a specific date. They may even direct them to set up a strategic management group to prepare the plan. It is also possible that the managers required to devise strategic plans are told to address specific strategic issues that have been identified by the top management team. The process of involvement in this case enables strategic plans to be better informed in terms of operating realities. It may also be hoped that the involvement will create more leadership at lower levels. Of course, the top managers cannot know for sure what kinds of strategic plans will be produced if they are trying to foster leadership. They are looking for these managers to use their judgement and initiative. But this is a price worth paying if it unleashes more leadership that can help with bringing about large-scale change programmes.

FORMAL INVOLVEMENT STRUCTURES

In some parts of the public sector which employ many professionals, employees have traditionally expected to have inputs in decision making. This can lead to the formation of committees for all sorts of matters, and much time spent in meetings. For example, a university may have an academic board, research committees, faculty boards, boards of study, and so on.

Management meetings and committee meetings may be used to ask for opinions about how the organisation and its activities should develop. However, such structures of committees and meetings can be seen as bureaucratic and mostly a waste of time. In some public sector organisations these structures are seen as holding up innovation and not particularly effective. More streamlined executive management structures are seen as better for getting things done. The persistence of bureaucratic committee structures and meetings alongside executive structures may be seen as mainly placating the feelings of professionals who value being involved in decision making. In universities academics may be elected to boards which act as the supreme policy-making body on academic affairs. The main initiative, however, usually lies with the vice-chancellor of the university and the senior management team. The university management structure, in fact, generally controls how committees at all level work and determines the issues that are routed through them. Collegiate arrangements appear to offer widespread involvement in planning change, but in practice it is the executive arrangements that are dominant in decision-making terms.

Professionals within public sector organisations are not always sanguine about the operation of the collegiate committees and meetings. There are complaints about time spent in too many meetings. There may be complaints about effectiveness of the committees and meetings. Professionals themselves may say that they are little more than 'talking shops'. There may be little action planning and little reporting back to constituencies within the organisation. There may be doubts about the representativeness of the individuals taking part in the meetings. Who are they speaking for?

Involving people through trade union channels has become less important in many public sector organisations—at least in the case of the UK. Trade unionism was strongly established in the public sector in the early decades after the Second World War. But after trade unions became weaker in the 1980s, more public sector managers began to stress the need to involve employees through non-trade-union channels as a means of building employee commitment. Collective bargaining and joint consultation procedures with trade unions continued to exist, but were not accorded the same degree of significance as they had enjoyed in the past. In some public sector organisations the decline in importance of union channels became evident when management decided to make people redundant despite union opposition. Unions in the public sector had been credited in the past with such power that making workers redundant in the face of union opposition would have been considered unthinkable. Well, the unthinkable has happened and unions have not been able to force commitment to full job security.

Some managers in the public sector are dissatisfied with the ability of trade unions to represent the complexity of their membership's interests and views. Trade unions have traditionally championed majority views and thus concentrated on translating a diverse and fluid set of views into a single coherent view on any matter under consideration. This can be attractive to management, but it can also be seen as oversimplifying issues and creating inflexibility. Management may experience this activity by unions as a constraint on change and innovation.

Of course, managers may also underestimate the degree to which trade unions help to surface attitudes and feelings that individuals are reluctant to express openly and directly to managers. In consequence, some managers appear to see unions as the source of their problems, and contrast the belligerence of union representatives with the reasonableness of the individual members of the union. In fact, unions help to make hidden problems visible, and thus make it possible for managers to address them.

INFORMAL INVOLVEMENT

In the light of a lack of confidence in bureaucratic meetings and committees to produce effective levels of involvement, public sector managers have been turning to informal processes of involvement. Chief executives in large public sector organisations have taken on the need to generate a sense of involvement, and they have done this directly and personally. Experienced chief executives have gone round their organisations on a frequent and regular basis to open up discussions with members of staff on the strategic direction of the organisation. They have gone round to talk about missions and values. They will spend time talking to groups of staff. And these are not pep talks. They ask the staff what they think and what their experiences have been.

The pep talk approach by the chief executive is little advocated. Many public sector organisations have large numbers of articulate professionals who do not respond to pep talks but who do like the chance to debate where the organisation is going. They like being treated with respect and expect that top managers will take the trouble to explain and seek to convince them. They do not like to be taken for granted.

Some chief executives in the public sector expect their staff to take some responsibility in finding out what is going on and then to contribute actively, and responsibly, to debates about future directions.

Temporary arrangements for informal groups or *ad hoc* meetings may be used to handle strategic changes. Volunteers from across the organisation may take part in discussions of proposals. Management is able to ask those present to react to outline ideas. This can be valuable in providing managers with opinion and feedback on future developments or changes, which they can then evaluate and develop as appropriate.

It is important to have a realistic view of informal and *ad hoc* groups. They do not work in isolation of political forces, they do not mean change is a completely friendly and harmonious phenomenon, and they have to engage formal procedures. A realistic view of informal methods and their place in the negotiation of change emerges from the study by Pettigrew et al. (1992) of strategic changes in the health services. One of their case studies looked at the development of proposals for the closure of a hospital and the redevelopment of St Mary's hospital in Paddington, London. The research certainly illustrated how informality may be used to develop strategic proposals. 'Internally, the style involved working with small groups, to tight deadlines, and finding ways round cumbersome NHS procedures' (p. 77). They suggest that one of the features explaining the acceptance of the proposals was the 'reduction of complexity through the use of *ad hoc* groups and winning the trust of those in the District [Health Authority] to pave the way for delegation' (p. 80).

But this study also shows how the proposals were developed in the context of lobbying for political support that was successful. They even managed to get a government minister to visit and express support. Their study also shows how power and interests were key factors in the acceptability of the proposals. It is reported that clinicians in St Mary's, Paddington, and the administrators formed a dominant coalition and that the 'victims' of change (i.e. clinicians at the hospital that was to be closed) were weak. It is reported that there had been a willingness to 'make concessions to permit other groups to buy into the strategy' (p. 80). So those shaping the strategic change proposals may have done some coalition building. Only after political lobbying and a small study group had produced a project report was formal consultation on proposals for rebuilding and service changes carried out.

Therefore, we can suggest three propositions that need to be addressed when using informal methods to involve managers and employees in thinking about and formulating proposals for visions and plans for strategic changes:

1.   There has to be external political support for the work.
2.   Those working in informal or *ad hoc* groups need to develop proposals that will produce or permit a critical mass of support in the wider organisation.
3.   The informal methods of generating proposals may be useful, but at some point have to link in to the formal decision-making procedures.

INVOLVEMENT IN PLANNING PROCESSES

Large-scale public sector organisations have brought in strategic planning processes and within these processes there are formal opportunities for staff involvement. Some organisations have facilitated workshops to enable cross-sections of employees to take part in generating the ideas for strategies to tackle specific issues. There have also been large-scale events to involve managers and employees directly in the deliberations to produce corporate strategic plans.

In addition, large organisations carry out strategic planning at different levels of the organisation and it is possible to encourage managers and employees at lower levels to work on the development of team plans. This allows, in modest ways, employees to be involved in planning their futures. In presenting their plans, these teams may arrive at dialogue with managers.

Corporate working parties and projects may be set up with formal terms of reference to work on parts of the strategic planning process. For example, groups of managers and employees from different parts of the organisation may be asked to work together and report back on corporate goals and priorities. The idea of using working parties and project teams is an attractive one. It offers prospects of breaking down departmental and status barriers that get in the way of corporate working. But there is a danger of overstretching the capacity of the organisation for such initiatives. This work is sometimes additional to the normal duties of participants, and although the work can tap the enthusiasm of people who like to participate, it can also be too much. Top managers have, therefore, to monitor the use of these mechanisms and use them judiciously.

Taking people with you can involve very complex planning arrangements. Bloomsbury DHA in the late 1980s involved clinicians through a complex structure in a process of formulating a strategy for rationalisation. There was a service planning group. Innumerable clinical advisory groups advised this. Through this machinery the district managed to develop a set of proposals to build a new hospital (Pettigrew et al. 1992, p. 96). The logic of such an approach is surely that investment in involving people pays off in better implementation.

SUMMARY AND CONCLUSIONS

In this chapter we have reviewed the reasons, nature, and methods of involving managers and employees in thinking about the future of public sector organisations. It has been argued that there are a number of rationales for involving people. It may help to get people to understand and commit themselves to strategic change. It can be useful in educating staff about the limits of what is politically acceptable. It may also be explained by a desire to empower managers and employees, with the aim of releasing the creativity and ingenuity of those who work in the organisation.

Reflecting these different rationales, involvement can have a range of forms. It may take the form of promoting top management views. It may be largely a process of dialogue between levels of the organisation. It may also be operationalised through delegated strategic planning powers.

The main methods of involvement include collegiate forms of meeting and committee work. These can be seen as bureaucratic and lacking in effectiveness and representativeness. The collegiate forms are also largely circumscribed or controlled by executive structures. There is a strong interest in the use of informal methods of achieving involvement of managers and employees, which can take the form of top managers making it their business to get out of their offices to visit groups of staff and ask them for views and experiences. It can also take the form of temporary groups or *ad hoc* meetings to discuss management proposals and obtain feedback.

Finally, the planning process offers opportunities for formally involving managers and employees. Facilitated workshops for cross-sections of employees and large-scale events to involve managers and employees directly in the deliberations to produce corporate strategic plans have both been used. Corporate working groups and project groups can be given responsibilities to carry out specific aspects of the strategic planning process. Then there are strategic planning systems that are designed to include planning processes at lower levels.

7

Installing Management

INTRODUCTION

This chapter concerns the need to develop or put in place managers and management systems to deepen leadership at all levels of an organisation. This is the final major aspect of leading strategic changes. Once the strategic vision has been formulated and managers and employees have been involved in thinking about the organisation's future, the main thing that has to be done is to ensure that there are managers who are required for the change activities of the next phase of strategic management.

This chapter begins with an examination of the reasons for installing management, including the reasons that managers are needed for corporate strategic working and to achieve the implementation of strategic change. The meaning of installing management is then explored. It will be seen that installing management means not only developing the necessary management personnel, but also developing management organisation and systems and techniques. Finally, the main processes by which management is installed are reviewed. Issues of training and development, recognition, and the allocation of responsibilities are all considered under methods of installing management.

THE IMPORTANCE OF MANAGEMENT

The rise of management in the public sector has been occurring for many years. Those who have risen up through the ranks of management have been engaged in creating a function quite distinct from the administrators that were their forerunners in the public sector. Making a clear distinction between the old administrators and the new managers of the public sector is possible on the basis of the underlying processes of administration and management. Administrators in the health services, local government, and other parts of the public sector were mainly engaging in processes that supported the roles of politicians and professionals. They implemented decisions and policies ultimately sanctioned by politicians and they enabled professionals to carry out a pre-eminent role in defining needs (within parameters set by legal mandates and the politicians' policies) and spending operational budgets.

Managers occupy a more pivotal role than did the administrators. Their role is seen as a more powerful and proactive one. They are more critical to the definition of public needs, which they champion and take an active role in determining by being in touch with the public. This may be referred to as increasing the 'responsiveness' of the public sector. They are more proactive in resourcing the activities of the public sector than were the old administrators. Many managers have taken on board the Osborne & Gaebler (1992) idea that public sector organisations should not just spend taxpayers' money; they also look for ways of acquiring resources through income generation. Finally, they are powerful in setting and managing performance targets.

Some commentators on the changes suggest that this is a managerialist agenda that involves less of a role for politicians. For example, Kakabadse et al. (1996, p. 394), who have made empirical comparisons between private and public managers, stress that changes in public sector management are down to governments:

> In essence, a succession of governments has challenged the traditional doctrine of public administration by adopting the position that public administration is more about the management of services and responsive implementation of policy than about policy development and design . . . This provoked the debate and dispute over the role of political judgement. On the one hand, the managerialist orientation is intended to provide for quicker and more community-responsive service orientation at the local level. On the other, democracy is driven to a place of lesser consequence, whereby the managerialist oriented administration slowly determines the parameters to the policy agenda.

The role of managers in performance management is sometimes given special emphasis. On this basis, it may be assumed that it is important to install management to ensure that public sector organisations perform better and achieve improved results. In Britain, local government, health services, education, and other public services brought in managers in a bid to increase efficiency. This is often seen as challenging the professionals and professional values and habits.

In some public sector organisations the middle and lower levels of management are recruited mainly from the ranks of professionals. This can cause concern to chief executives and their executive team. The top tiers of management may be seen as thoroughly competent and quite clear about the responsibilities and tasks of management. They may be seen as dedicated and effective. However, at the middle and first level the individuals may be seen as too professional in their outlook. They may be perceived as lacking a commitment to management, and as lacking the expertise and instincts of a manager. They have not been trained as managers and their effectiveness as managers may be rated as very uneven. In the health services these managers are professional doctors, paramedical personnel, nurses, and others. These are people who are trying to reconcile their occupational identities. Are they professionals who manage people? Or are they managers with a professional background? In local government the managers are social workers, planners, environmental health officers, and so on. In universities and schools they are academics and teachers. This suggests the managerialist agenda is not just about displacing an administrative culture, but also about replacing professional personnel by 'proper' managers.

A second but possibly related rationale for installing management is the need for public sector organisations to keep up with the increasing rate of change. Health services, local public services, education are all changing. Politicians have imposed most of the change. Performance management systems, structural reorganisations, cross-boundary working are some examples of the changes. This creates issues for public sector organisations. Managers are needed to help adapt the organisations to cope. The general perception is that this external change is becoming more and more rapid. Managers are needed who can turn this imposed change into innovation. Managers who are resourceful and can handle the accelerating change are becoming more essential.

The impact of governments that are pro-public services but have demanding expectations has given this impetus to install management a new twist. Instead of the public sector being under pressure from governments that are ideologically opposed to public services, in a number of countries the governmental pressure on the public services is for modernising. There is thus a need for managers who can act as agents of the modernising agenda.

A very important reason for installing management from the point of view of this book is the need to develop corporate strategic working. The use of strategic planning to ensure that public sector organisations are properly aligned with official mandates, are operating on an efficient and streamlined basis, and are purposefully preparing themselves for the future, is still relatively new. In many organisations the work of corporate strategic planning is being carried out by a very small number of senior managers. Chief executives in recent years have wanted to deepen the involvement of their organisations in corporate strategic management. Instead of a handful of senior managers, they would like to see 30 or 50 or more managers drawn into working effectively on strategic planning. For whatever reason, they have felt that their organisations were short on effective middle–senior managers for corporate strategic management purposes. They have thought that more capable managers needed to be brought on, managers who were good retained, and current middle managers needed more training and development.

Chief executives have needed to develop middle and front-line managers for strategy implementation, not just for formulation of strategic plans. Especially where organisations employed large numbers of professionals, there was a need for middle managers who could persist at the implementation tasks. The professionals were sceptical of strategy because they could see the shortage of managers able and willing to work patiently at making sure the strategic plans were put into practice.

Furthermore, the failure to implement strategic plans meant that shortages of capable managers committed to corporate strategic management processes meant that some organisations were failing to deliver their intentions of providing better services to the public. At the end of the day, the chief executives in these public sector organisations were concerned about the shortages and deficiencies in management because they meant that they were not providing better services for the public as demanded by politicians.

MIDDLE AND FRONT-LINE MANAGEMENT PEOPLE

In UK public services since the 1980s, organisations have been trying to get the right people into management positions. This has meant first identifying and highlighting a tier of management. In some organisations this could amount to 50 or 60 middle-tier jobs. In larger organisations this could mean hundreds of management jobs. It has then meant sifting through the current managers. Who is performing well? Who is performing less than satisfactorily? Who was capable of shouldering responsibility, and who was not? It has meant making judgements about how many needed more training and support to perform well and how many were unsuited to being managers. People in the last category have found the job of managing more and more stressful as the expectations of top management increased. Some left and found jobs elsewhere; some chose or accepted demotion. In these ways, over a period of years, organisations sorted out their middle managers. There are organisations now where the chief executive believes that the body of middle managers is made up of good managers and that they are getting support and encouragement to provide effective leadership at middle-management level.

Organisations vary in how they achieve the placing of the right people in middle and front-line management. Some believe the talents potentially exist in the present body of managers, but that training and development programmes are needed to bring out latent abilities. Others see the problem more in terms of the right and wrong people. They have a policy of getting the right people by being ruthless and producing high attrition rates among the managers who are wrong for the organisation. One local authority chief executive reckoned that at the time they began to improve their management they had about one in six of the key tier of middle managers who were not up to the requirements of the role. Another chief executive explained that the issue was whether the individual manager subscribed to the conception of management—not whether they were personally capable. 'It's like the old British Airways experience, it's probably bad to cite today, when they had their big reorganisation in the 80s some pretty good people left there, but they were wrong. Well, we have to do the same thing.'

We can in these different approaches perceive an expression of the old nurture–nature debate. Are good managers made or born? Of course, organisations may get the middle and front-line management they want by a combination of nurture and nature methods.

The top managers of public sector organisations have constructed (in their minds or on paper) ideal profiles of the effective middle and front-line manager. These vary from one organisation to another. One chief executive from a hospital described his profile for managers as follows. They are people who do things rigorously. On the other hand they have a strong emotional feeling for the services they manage. They have to be good at working with professionals, meaning both that they can be decisive when dealing with professionals and that they command their respect. In other words, they need to be able to exercise authority over professionals. This is crucial. If they cannot work with professionals in this way, then they cannot effectively do the job. They have to be good at corporate working. This means that they are able to balance the corporate priorities with the more local service ones. This requires skills in conflict resolution. Finally, they have to be effective in cross-boundary working. The effective hospital manager is expected by this chief executive to work in partnership with department managers in local authority social services and other organisations. This entails making judgements about when to work laterally through partnerships and when to refer matters up the management line of the hospital.

For example, a general manager in medicine within a hospital needs to work with the local authority social services, general practitioners, and community trusts. Some of this cross-boundary management is about improving the co-ordination of public services. There has, for instance, been a great effort to improve support for patients coming into and leaving hospital care.

It was interesting that for this chief executive the first thing on the profile of the effective manager was doing things rigorously. This chief executive put a great emphasis on the need for precision and correctness in management. He felt that too many managers lacked an attention to detail. He was concerned that there were many ambitious managers in the UK's NHS who are good at thinking but temperamentally poorly equipped to deal with the detail. Indeed, he links this to a lack of interest in implementation. Having done the thinking they very quickly lose interest in implementing the ideas. It is easy to imagine how unsatisfactory this may seem to top managers who may feel that they handle the visionary stuff and need good middle and front-line managers to take responsibility for ensuring that strategic visions and plans are implemented throughout the services.

The middle and front-line managers of the new public sector are meant to be corporate minded. When new managers are appointed, the interview panels are looking for people who will work corporately. Managers who hold a primary allegiance to a department rather than the whole organisation are rejected. The new corporate-minded manager has been recruited to spearhead a fresh start for the public sector. They are seen as the champions of innovation in service delivery. They are expected to be working together across departmental boundaries with the aim of improving services and supporting the efforts of top management to achieve innovation and creativity.

MANAGEMENT ORGANISATION

Installing management is also about installing management organisation. For most of the 1980s and 1990s public sector organisations have tended to install devolved or decentralised management. In the UK the message of Peters & Waterman's (1982) *In Search of Excellence* was taken to heart—especially ideas about the best organisational form. They advocated small headquarter staffs and operational decentralisation. Within a couple of years, by the mid 1980s, Wrekin District Council and the London Borough of Hammersmith and Fulham were using the ideas of Peters and Waterman and the Audit Commission was referring to the ideas in publications. Pioneering councils like Kirklees became known in the 1990s as innovative, something that was attributed to their devolved service delivery arrangements, as well as their focus on issues by the top level of management. In the early 1990s newly formed health trusts like Kings' Healthcare in London's Denmark Hill drew up blueprints for their new organisations based on decentralised management. In summary, public sector organisations of different kinds reduced the size of central departments (such as personnel) and devolved responsibilities down to line managers. Middle tiers of management were thinned. Values were enunciated as a way of providing control while devolving power down the management line. Chief executives and top managers talked about the way they had loosened their control systems.

Therefore, top management has been creating a capacity for organisational leadership at all levels by installing decentralised or devolved management. Many chief executives have worked on developing the management structure underneath the top management. They have slimmed down middle management as a way of reducing the tendency to top-down control by hierarchical structures. With less middle management in the structure they have hoped that front-line service managers have more discretion over budgets, personnel practices, and service delivery. These efforts have been accompanied by flattening of structures. This has meant widening the span of control of managers, which theoretically underpins a less controlling style of superior–subordinate management line. Top management teams were radically slimmed so that a chief executive often ended up with only three or four directors in their management team. In the past local authority chief executives had much bigger management teams. One London borough, for example, used to have a team of 10 or 11 'chief officers'; this was slimmed down.

The intended consequence of slimming down middle management, creating small top management teams, and devolving power over budgets and people was meant to be that front-line service managers were given more responsibility and were encouraged in risk taking, and creativity. Not all of the more senior managers liked to relinquish control of budgets and staffing. There were also fewer career opportunities for many managers as a result of the changes. But chief executives and their supporters (especially elected politicians) pushed through changes in order to empower the front-line service managers and hoped that they would respond by taking the initiative. One chief executive recently said, 'I think it's wrong that the centre should seek to dictate the whole raft of things that might go on in an organisation that is 4000 people strong. In doing that you probably stop some really clever stuff that may not look very good on the outset but because of the persistence of some individuals might actually get there.' Public sector chief executives have urged support for managers doing innovative things, and worried about managers who did not use their initiative and did nothing. Maverick figures became more acceptable because they might break up the corporate uniformity of past practices.

The chief executives who were not happy just to let front-line managers and professionals act with complete autonomy have put effort into instilling a strong sense of purpose so that devolving management would produce the outcomes required. Business planning and seminars and management development processes were used to ensure that devolved management worked in line with corporate intentions. One hospital, for example, has been in the habit of taking 100 people away together—away for a day—to debate corporate issues and strategic intentions.

The changes in the management structures had implications for the way that elected politicians and boards operated in the public sector. At a trivial level, it might be noted that politicians had to be persuaded not only to support changes in management organisation. They also had to formulate or endorse statements of corporate values and visions. But there were also changes for the boards that governed hospitals and governing bodies of universities. These boards had to operate differently as chief executives had changed how they operated.

A very serious question that emerges after many years of installing devolved management structures concerns the performance of such structures. Even if they have delivered innovation, have they also delivered performance and results as judged by the public? There are signs that the hands-off approach of devolved structures can leave top management with few levers or mechanisms for delivering high performance as well as creative organisations. The chief executive may feel that core values and visions have been useful in fostering a focus on front-line managers, but how well does it deliver on public consultation, corporate strategic planning, and joined-up government? If hierarchical management has had its day, and the limits of the devolved form of management are being reached, what new types of corporate management arrangements are needed?

MANAGEMENT SYSTEMS AND TECHNIQUES

Effective management is not just a matter of the right people and the right structure. Public sector organisations have been bringing in management systems and techniques such as quality management, performance management, and teamworking. There has been widespread uptake of the business excellence model and benchmarking techniques, and business process engineering stirred a lot of interest for a while.

These systems and techniques have been important for creating higher standards. A number of public sector organisations brought in quality management approaches in the early 1990s. Perhaps the employment of large numbers of professionals in the past meant that external training and professional development of professionals were assumed to take care of quality concerns. But, with the rise of managerialism in the public sector, a deliberate approach was seen as necessary. Some organisations have enthusiastically seized on the European excellence model. This is largely based on a self-assessment. It has some obvious potential for diagnosing the causes of performance deficits and thus could be seen as a useful management tool for setting improvement goals as part of a performance management system.

Many organisations have also brought in more powerful or sophisticated systems for individual service planning, budgeting linked to strategic priorities (e.g. priority-based budgeting), staff appraisals for setting personal objectives and planning training and development, and consulting the public. There has been some interest, for example in higher education, in improving knowledge management systems.

AN ECOLOGICAL VIEW OF INSTALLING MANAGEMENT

Some chief executives have an ecological view of how an organisation ends up with the managers it employs. They point out that there is always some level of turnover among managers in most organisations. Managers retire. Managers find jobs with other organisations. If the organisation is trying to survive in a very tough environment, they may feel that the managers who are not up to the challenges are the ones most likely to leave. The conclusion is that the quality of management improves in the face of a tough environment. (There are other ecological views that say you lose the best managers if the organisation is too bureaucratic and stifles them, or if the organisation is in trouble and needs its best managers because they are the ones who find it easiest to get another job.)

This can lead to an assessment of the management survivors as being those who are well adapted to the new conditions. They are adapted, for example, to more demanding political pressures, managing with less while doing more, and able to work in a variety of ways (outsourcing as well as partnership working, enabling as well as regulating, consulting the public as well as listening to the elected representatives of the electorate). As one chief executive put it, the survivors 'still come to work with a smile on their face, and still keep looking for ways of delivering services'.

In consequence some chief executives feel content with their managers. They see them as optimistic, proactive, and willing to work in a corporate way with managers from other services. The survivors know that commitment and creativity are the only way to survive as managers, and it is no use complaining about the resource constraints.

Does this ecological view mean that top management has nothing to do but leave a volatile and challenging environment to create through attrition the managers they need? Not all top management with an ecological analysis is prepared to be totally passive. Some top managers feel they have a role to play in spotting the managers that are better adapted to the new conditions. A chief executive keeps an eye on how well his or her managers are doing, and if a manager is doing well, then he or she puts more opportunities their way. So, they decide who deserves a chance to take on bigger management projects or jobs.

The top managers who hold an ecological view may tend to be sceptical about the benefits of training courses for managers. They may be doubtful of the value of training rather than completely dismissive. On the other hand, some top managers may feel that the ecological processes need a bit of a helping hand. Those who have survived because they are better adapted may still need some finishing off in terms of knowledge and skills. This may require formal training courses, or systems to help managers carry out their own personal development.

TRAINING AND DEVELOPMENT

Training and development programmes are an obvious way in which to create the management needed for leading strategic changes at all levels of the organisation. Some organisations will employ their own specialist staff to design and even deliver such programmes. The programmes may concentrate on ensuring that managers are fully conversant with corporate policies. They can try to develop skills in handling staff issues. They may cover the legal aspects of recruiting and selecting staff. They may cover leadership and planning skills. Other matters that may be covered include financial management, quality, customer service, health and safety, and equal opportunities.

The usual concern about in-house corporate programmes is that they will lack interest for the participants. Managers may be put on courses, find them irrelevant to their everyday problems, and experience their delivery as dull. Managers may feel that their boss's suggestion that they should attend the course is an implied criticism. If attendance of all middle managers is compulsory, they may feel that they are being 'sheep dipped', with top management trying to hammer in some 'messages' via the trainers. The managers who attend them do not always react enthusiastically to corporate courses.

Management programmes may be designed for specific layers of management to raise awareness about issues selected by top management as critical. Workshops, away days, and short courses may be designed to develop this awareness and help managers to think about how to avoid problems and handle matters.

'Away days' are particularly useful for attempting to bring about attitudinal changes among managers. These events provide favourable conditions for engaging middle managers in discussion and debate. This can challenge existing ways of looking at things and allow managers to think through the implications of new policies. Edicts from top management or simple pep talks are much less effective in bringing about reconceptualisations and attitude shifts.

In recent years there have also been attempts to improve public sector managers by using programmes designed to assess performance competence and award management qualifications. Bradford Council in the north of England, for example, recently decided to place 30 middle managers every year on a programme leading to a national vocational qualification. These are not necessarily also training programmes, but even processes of compiling portfolios of evidence for assessment purposes can be educational. The process of assessment can encourage experienced managers to reflect on their experiences and they may find this encourages a further development of capability. However, there is little if any rigorous evidence to demonstrate that such vocational assessments improve management.

There are at least three points that are important to consider in designing management development approaches in the public sector. First, if management development programmes are aimed at increasing the knowledge, awareness, and skills of individual managers, how will they meet organisational needs? For example, how effective are programmes developing individual managers for promoting corporate-minded managers? Just because managers from different departments have all been on the same standard course, will this mean that they are more inclined to identify with the organisation as a whole? Or do they need training and developing in corporate working skills specifically?

Secondly, if it is decided that the organisation as a whole needs managers with more skills in, say planning and consulting the public, how is the timing of the training and development linked to organisational changes? There is no point in training large numbers of middle and front-line managers in budgetary control and financial management issues if budgetary control and financial management are very centralised. The timing of training should be synchronised with the delegation of budgetary authority. But if the organisation fears the loosening of this control and errors in budget management, and has no intention of delegating control in the foreseeable future, then there is no point in providing the training.

Thirdly, if top managers are keen to use training and development to raise levels of awareness about corporate issues among middle and front-line managers, it is important that they make explicit how they expect this increased awareness will benefit the organisation. What are they expecting middle and front-line managers to do with this new level of awareness? Have they got the resources, commitment, or mandate to do anything with it?

RECOGNISING GOOD WORK OF MANAGERS

Developing managers and management organisation is not just done by formal management development programmes. Senior managers have realised that delegation of decision making down the management line involves developing the confidence of managers.

Front-line managers must feel confident that they will be supported in their use of budgets to be innovative and improve the results. The idea of celebrating the 'good news' that results from delegation is widely appreciated. This is one way of building confidence.

This policy of building confidence by celebrating and acknowledging the efforts of front-line managers has to be executed consistently, and in relation to very small successes as well as big wins. This is the way that chief executives and senior managers have been trying to create the right environment for developing managers who will use their initiative and drive the organisation's performance.

This confidence building can be stage managed in management conferences or managers' forums for the organisation's middle managers. If these are held on a regular basis, then these are major platforms for chief executives to highlight successes of middle and front-line managers. This public recognition is believed to be highly motivating for middle and front-line managers.

REDESIGNING RESPONSIBILITIES

Training and recognition are probably best seen as adjuncts to processes of redesigning responsibilities. Although it has been suggested that devolved or decentralised management structures may have reached their limits of usefulness, it is also instructive to look at how even these require systematic redesign of responsibilities within management. If senior managers do not change, they may neutralise attempts to empower service managers. Chief executives may have to tell directors who have been very 'hands on' in managing services that they have new responsibilities for managing strategic issues and partnership working with other organisations. If the directors fail to take up these new responsibilities there may be a temptation for them to exercise close monitoring of service managers. This can be so intrusive that policies of decentralisation are foiled.

Some managers adapt more quickly to new responsibilities than others. Some directors have been reluctant to adapt to decentralisation and have resisted and delayed the delegation of budget management.

The discussions of the design of management responsibilities in the public sector can be somewhat simplistic. It is sometimes tacitly assumed that either there is an allocation of responsibilities based on a centralised design, or an allocation based on a decentralisation model. Some organisations, however, have tried to create more complex structures. The top management team has not taken a 'hands off' approach with respect to service delivery and taken up a pure strategic management role. It has retained some control for service delivery and budgetary control. Other patterns for allocating responsibilities between tiers of management can be imagined, providing the various responsibilities are identified. The problem may be that commentators have lumped responsibilities under two broad categories, service delivery and strategic. But top management and service management responsibilities might be more finely broken down than this. For example, who is responsible for identifying desirable organisational and management capabilities and which part of the organisation is responsible for developing them? Which part is responsible for allocating resources (human, financial, etc.) to develop capabilities? Which part of the organisation is responsible for setting the cost and quality parameters of a new activity? Which part is responsible for forging working partnerships? Who is responsible for identifying community issues that require problem-solving activities? Who should be responsible for monitoring performance and deciding on improvement goals? And so on. Perhaps the simple argument about centralised versus decentralised management structures is too crude.

There are mechanisms and techniques for discussing and agreeing responsibilities among managers. While the overall principles of allocating responsibilities between tiers of management may be decided by the chief executive and the top management team (with the support of politicians), this needs to be carried through in detailed planning. Thorough consultation can be useful if the planning of responsibilities is to be effective. One chief executive of a hospital was an enthusiastic supporter of a process of clarifying responsibilities by systematically covering all the major units of the hospital using a technique called responsibility charting. This clarifies who is responsible for a decision, who has a right to veto a decision, who must put resources towards implementing the decision, and who has a right to be informed. This charting can be done by a group of all those who are affected, and should result in agreed allocation of responsibilities.

SUMMARY AND CONCLUSIONS

This chapter has completed an examination of the activities important for the ability of the organisation to deliver the leadership of
strategic change. The reasons for installing and deepening management were considered. The issue was placed in the context of the rise
of management in the public sector, and the demise of an older
administrative culture. The association of the rise of the importance
of management with pressures to change and modernise the public
sector was noted. Most important of all, however, the rationale for
management in terms of corporate working, effective implementation of strategic change and the provision of better services to the
public was advanced.

The different aspects of installing management were examined.
They can be seen as obtaining and developing the personnel to
occupy middle and front-line management positions, shaping the
management organisation, and the application of management systems and techniques. It was noted that many public sector organisations have been absorbed in the task of devolving management and
creating decentralised management structures. The continuing wisdom of this has been questioned. In the light of the modernisation
agenda, with its emphasis on consulting the public, achieving better
results, and partnership working, there may need to be some innovation in management structures for the public sector.

Finally, the chapter outlined the different methods of forming
middle and front-line management. There was a brief note on ecological processes and how top managers may support them. Then
the chapter reviewed the use of training and encouragement. The
chapter finished with a brief consideration of the design of structures
and allocating management responsibilities.

8

Engaging Others in the Organisation with the Vision or Strategic Intent

INTRODUCTION

Implementing strategic visions and their associated strategic plans involves many important activities and processes. Three are especially important concerns for chief executives and senior managers. These are engaging others in the organisation with the vision or strategic intent; focusing and aligning the organisation; and stabilising changes and ensuring that performance targets are achieved.

We concentrate on the first of these in this chapter. This is a different process from involving others in thinking about the future. In the implementation phase of strategic change top managers are expecting lower-level managers and employees to act in accordance with the strategic vision and strategic plans. 'As plans evolve and action plans begin to emerge, middle and lower levels of management are brought on board . . . At the appropriate time, all line employees must become involved and come to understand their part in the implementation of the plan' (Bushnell & Halus 1992, p. 365). No matter how widely top managers have consulted the members of the organisation when forming the strategic vision and intent, it is never enough to ensure that everybody feels in complete accord with the vision and plans. Furthermore, a strategic plan only produces results by people working at its implementation. Bushnell & Halus (1992) cite Peter Drucker's views that a plan is only good intentions until it 'degenerates' into work and that there is a need for key people to become committed to working on specific tasks. Therefore, top managers need lower-level managers to learn about the strategic vision and plan, to feel committed to them, to support them, and act in ways to help their implementation. Therefore, at this point, there must be an effort to get people to engage with the strategic vision and intent.

In this chapter we look at the reasons top managers have for wishing to engage others with the strategic vision or intent. Then the nature of the process is considered. For some top managers engaging people is about getting minds and emotions centred on the strategic change. Others see engaging people as getting them interested and enthusiastic. Some are inclined to see it in behavioural terms. They see engaging members of the organisation in change as about aligning their actions with the strategic vision and intent. Finally, the methods used to produce higher levels of engagement with the strategic vision and intent are explored—communication exercises, involvement processes, approaches that rely on formal systems, and the use of symbolic approaches.

WHY ENGAGE OTHERS?

Of course, top managers want all members of the organisation to understand strategic changes and the need for changes, and then to become committed wholeheartedly to making the changes. The top managers make efforts to communicate the intended changes to people in the organisation, but generally know that the results will be mixed in terms of the reactions of managers and employees. They may, and probably will, encounter some resistance.

Resistance may take the form of open conflict (even industrial action). It may take the form of passive resistance. Employees may claim not to have been informed of the changes required. They may simply ignore new policies hoping that nobody will be along to check whether they are complying. They may just drag their feet. They may do a lot of moaning and complaining.

The problem of resistance may be conceptualised by managers as being a communication problem—communications by top management having failed to convince people to support the changes. There could be various explanations for the failure of communication by top managers. Organisations rarely check systematically how well communication systems work. Perhaps top managers have not spent enough time talking to managers and employees. Perhaps they have not been good at convincing them that the situation requires such changes.

Top managers in the public sector will also blame conservative attitudes and expectations among managers and employees. Many managers (in the private as well as the public sector) take the view that the 'natural instinct' of people is to resist new ideas and changes in their organisation. They suggest that people are naturally conservative. Some top managers in the public sector go further than this and see resistance to change as peculiarly virulent in large public sector organisations. Top managers meeting resistance from professional employees often say this. They note that professional employees in particular will couch their objections to change as rooted in a 'principled position'. Changes instigated by top management may require changed working methods to achieve higher levels of productivity. They may involve changes in who receives the service. Professionals may then see themselves as defending 'standards' of service or the rights of sections of the public. Top managers may feel little sympathy for the 'principled' objections of professional employees and feel frustrated with the resistance. The resistance is perceived as just holding up necessary change and progress.

Why should professionals have conservative attitudes and expectations? The occupational training and socialisation of professionals may be blamed. In some cases the turf wars between professional groups may be seen as aggravating the conservatism. So professionals may be seen as innately conservative in their attitudes and expectations.

But professionals are not so easily dismissed by all managers in the public sector. One hospital chief executive recently stressed the intellectual calibre of his professional staff. He said, 'An organisation such as this has a lot of very high calibre intellects within it, and the bulk of its staff are pretty intelligent. But what you find is, in terms of understanding, a blockage in terms of expectation which has to be changed.' He was, however, confident that engaging professionals in thinking about the changes required by a strategy was the right way forward. In his opinion, professionals may be conservative, but rational debate and discussion about strategy and change could usually produce agreement and understanding.

Some managers are not looking for total success in overcoming or avoiding resistance. If the politicians or governing body are putting managers under a lot of pressure to make changes, or if the top managers themselves are determined to make changes, then they may feel that their best option is to get sufficient co-operation that they can make progress. They will try to engage the 'average' employee so that they get a critical mass of support. There may still be discontented voices among the employees, but they will seek sufficient support to make changes without causing all-out conflict. If they do not try to engage them, then the groups of employees most opposed to the changes may persuade the 'floating voters' to oppose the changes.

On the other hand, it is interesting how many top managers are not content with achieving mere compliance with strategic decisions. Chief executives who want to make strategic changes are expecting enthusiasm and 'energy' from all members of the organisation—not just their immediate team of top managers. They expect enthusiasm and commitment even when they know this is not forthcoming. This is a normative expectation: they feel people should be enthusiastic. It is not a statement of what actually is expected. A local government chief executive emphasised the importance of people in the organisation believing in strategy: 'And they have got to believe it. But if you have got people who are cynical, who are sending it up, who are saying it's never going to happen, or who are simply ignoring it . . .'

UNIFYING THE ORGANISATION

Sometimes public sector managers worry about how they can best keep people in the organisation working together and keep the organisation from fragmenting. A popular answer for many years has been the need to create a shared vision of the future. Consequently, top managers may approve communication and training exercises or initiatives to instigate a shared vision or remind everybody in the organisation what the vision is. Less frequently, top managers believe that a consensus about a strategic vision comes as a result of a process of debate.

The absence of a shared strategic vision may be seen as the fault of poor leadership that fails to inspire staff with a strategic vision. Chief executives who have a low-key style of leading are sometimes criticised for not being more visionary. There are other sources of problems that receive less attention. Organisations that have several professional groupings (for example, hospitals and local authorities) can also suffer from tensions due to professional differences. If different units or departments are controlled or heavily influenced by a particular professional group, then the unit or department's goals can easily come to reflect professional interests. This is the basis of intra-organisational conflicts as well as creating problems for unity around corporate strategic targets. Professional rivalry creates internal tensions, especially in relation to the competition for resources. There are even conflicts within professional groups (e.g. between medical specialities) in large complex hospitals. The tensions are volatile in the sense that there are constant changes in the composition of coalitions as the competition for resources evolves.

MOBILISING THE ORGANISATION'S BIGGEST RESOURCE

Many chief executives in the public sector have tended in recent years to see budget allocations as important but people as the key resource. To quote a local government chief executive: 'I take the view that there are 9000 people working for this organisation. It's the biggest single resource the organisation has got.'

If people are the key resource then it is important that top management spends an appropriate amount of time trying to create the conditions in which they are thinking, feeling, and behaving in a way that maximises the value delivered to the public. Action that gets employees and managers engaged with the strategic vision and that achieves support for the strategic plan is obviously a top priority.

DEFINING HIGH LEVELS OF ENGAGEMENT

Some top managers look for very high levels of engagement. They want people to be committed to the strategic vision. They want their emotions as well as their mind engaged with the strategic changes. A chief executive who strongly approves of strategic management expressed his organisation's experience of this as follows: 'Strategic management was able to engage peoples' minds and to an extent their emotions in the whole idea of change.' They are keen to take managers and employees with them on the journey of strategic change.

Others also want people to engage with strategic change, but there is a substantially lower expectation that people will make an intense personal commitment. They are looking for enthusiasm and interest, rather than hearts and minds. Top managers may look to middle tiers of management to generate this enthusiasm and interest among employees. They will know that not all middle managers will be effective in this process and that engagement with strategic change will not be consistently developed throughout the organisation. Alternatively, top managers may identify a key senior manager to be responsible for the management of change, and this person will have a small team to help develop the skills and readiness for strategic change. This model has been tried at the Tate Gallery, an organisation that has been developing and changing a great deal in recent years.

Finally, there are top managers who, if asked, would tend to define engagement largely in behavioural terms. They, tacitly, view engagement of people with strategic change as a logical process of getting people to act in alignment with mission, strategic vision, and strategic plans. Their organisations may have a corporate statement that sets out the strategic direction. Ideally, people in the organisation act to implement the strategic vision and plans.

COMMUNICATING THE STRATEGIC VISION

The strategic vision by an organisation's top management could be implemented by asking department or unit managers to submit strategic and operational plans that are integrated with the strategic vision. Or top managers could set up strategic projects. In the process of implementing the strategic vision in these and other ways the strategic vision and the associated plan will be communicated. However, organisations may want a special communications exercise to disseminate the strategic vision and plan throughout the organisation. Such an exercise presents to managers and employees a picture of what the future might be and what is expected of employees. This is often described in terms of communicating key 'messages' to managers and employees.

One chief executive described communicating as a two-step process. The first step is when the organisation turns the strategic plan into a 'message', which he defined as comprising ideas of where the organisation is, where management is intending it to go, and what contribution is expected of members of the organisation. The second is delivering the message through a communication exercise. Messages may also be signalled through behaviour. For example, a unit general manager was appointed to Rainhill Hospital (England) in the mid 1980s. He signalled his seriousness about implementing the closure of the hospital by closing wards soon after his appointment (Pettigrew et al. 1992, p. 163).

One reason for organising a special communication exercise is that it is important to get the balance right between sending clear expectations based on the strategic vision and, at the same time, preparing people to handle the uncertainties of change. This involves motivating people to cope with the inevitable adjustments and refinements that are needed if the core strategic vision is going to benefit from the increasing knowledge resulting from the process of implementation.

Designing a communication exercise requires some tricky choices to be made. For example, there are problems in communicating strategic vision to various levels of public sector organisations. Should the same message be given to everybody or should top management ensure messages are tailored to suit different levels of the organisation? Do those who are on the front line of service delivery require messages delivered more confidently and with greater certainty? Can senior and middle managers tolerate messages with more ambiguities?

Top management teams sometimes turn to human resource management specialists and ask them to design induction courses for new starters and training courses for all staff to communicate the organisation's strategic vision and plans. The top managers will want the human resource specialists to concentrate on getting the key messages to as many members of staff as possible. Indeed, the desire of top management to foster support for strategic changes can prompt them to become strong supporters of induction courses for new starters as vehicles for communicating key messages. Therefore, either organisations develop corporate induction courses, or modify existing ones, to ensure that new starters hear about where the organisation is going, what the big strategic goals are, and what contribution the organisation expects from employees. The chief executive may even speak on induction courses and personally try to persuade employees of the importance of strategic change for the future of the organisation.

One chief executive in a large public sector organisation has a policy of meeting all new starters in their first week. This meeting takes place in the chief executive's office. The new starters are invited to sit down and there is a discussion. The chief executive sees this as a very effective way of helping to make the induction of each individual into the organisation memorable. He hopes that the meeting will shape each individual's subsequent career in the organisation. Although meeting all new starters is time consuming, the chief executive relishes the enthusiasm that he finds and considers the time well spent.

Human resource specialists may also put on courses for other staff. The training courses in one organisation cover both the corporate values and the corporate plan. The training course is described as seeking to communicate corporate plan and department and section objectives as clearly as possible. Another way of communicating to managers and employees is by mass meetings. Top managers, and politicians, may speak to mass meetings on a regular basis. In one organisation, the mass meetings take place twice a year in all the main buildings.

Some organisations have formal communication systems that can be used to communicate strategic visions and corporate strategic plans. These systems may comprise briefing meetings, departmental meetings, and staff meetings. In the case of formal communication systems, top managers may worry about how well the organisation is able to cascade messages down the organisation. Even with formal systems, it is difficult to ensure that all managers play their part conscientiously in briefing systems to convey the messages. Even if they do, messages are translated as they go down the management line. The results may be disappointing for top managers.

Communications are not just targeted on employees. Some chief executives put a great deal of effort into talking to management groups. Many organisations in recent years have formally recognised the existence of a management constituency and have created management forums. In large organisations, 200 or 300 managers might attend these forums. In summary, public sector organisations have a variety of options for communicating key messages about strategic visions and plans. Those considered above are mainly one-way. They all, in some sense, involve rolling out or cascading messages. Top managers may indeed see this as what is required. Having decided on a strategic direction they may look to effective communication to ensure all managers and employees are engaged with the strategic changes they have planned. However, even in successful organisations, top managers must realise that it is hard to achieve consensus by rolling out visions and values and cascading key messages.

DIALOGUE

One-way communications and cascading messages have their limitations as methods of engaging managers and employees with planned strategic changes. An alternative approach is to set up a dialogue with managers and employees. This is harder, but the rewards in terms of levels of engagement may be greater.

A public sector organisation can design a programme for creating dialogue with managers and employees about the strategic vision, plans, and values of the organisation. The aim is to create a climate of debate. Top managers will be pleased if such a programme makes strategic change a hot topic for discussion and debate. Such a programme may involve top managers meeting staff on a frequent basis, presenting their ideas for the future of the organisation, and asking staff what they think of it. Do they like it? What do they not like about it? What is missing? This interactive process, if designed well, enables staff to feed back their experience and opinion. However, unless top managers not only listen to staff, but also learn from them, then it is not dialogue but really a top-down communication. Therefore, this requires that the chief executive and top managers are tolerant of challenging views and interested in using dialogue processes to improve the quality of strategic thinking. In a dialogue process the top managers have some hopes of advising and influencing staff and also of creating a consensus based on the power of arguments and evidence. However, it is important to make the point, again, that top managers have to be transparent in their learning from dialogue. They must also be prepared to discuss the issues raised by staff and about budgetary issues. Some chief executives have been pleasantly surprised by the experiences of engaging in real dialogue with staff. Some will admit that they are surprised by the subjects that are of interest to staff and their understanding of the constraints and pressures on the organisation. They frankly admit that they expected little in the way of ideas from employees. However, they discover that employees do have ideas for making the organisation better.

INVOLVING STAFF TO ENGAGE STAFF

Employees can be engaged through involvement schemes. One approach is to involve staff by consulting them on the top managers' strategic vision and plans. This is thought to spread engagement with the strategy and maybe even ownership of the strategy.

It is sometimes argued that offering professional employees the opportunity to be involved in strategy can motivate them in particular. However, it is probable that other employees are no different from professionals in this respect—they probably also like being asked their opinion. Employees in the first flush of being consulted may be prepared not to only offer their opinion but also act enthusiastically to help realise the strategic changes. But employees soon see through phoney consultation. Thus, consultation must have an impact, otherwise a temporary increase in employee enthusiasm soon gives way to cynicism and even resentment.

Managers listening to employees is only the first step. The next requirement is that there is a successful outcome. Everybody likes to be associated with success. If employees give managers the benefit of the doubt and respond positively to an invitation to be involved, and if the result is a successful strategy, then the consultation receives positive reinforcement. As a result, there may be a growing sense of confidence and mutual respect between managers and employees in the organisation.

The importance of management achieving successful outcomes may have a special significance in the health services where the training of doctors and paramedical professionals contains a scientific element. For this scientific training could influence the culture of professionals in hospitals and affect how they respond to managers. One chief executive implied that trust in the strategic planning of managers is conditioned by a scientific scepticism. He took the view that engaging people with a strategic vision is about much more than having a debate:

> It's partly about debate. But much more importantly is actually doing it. The reason being that the abiding culture of places such as this is that [management action] is evaluated. The tendency is towards being scientific. And so their judgement is much better placed, not on what you say will be done . . . but what has been done and what can be measured. If you can then say what has been done and . . . then relate it to say, well we said in fact we would do this, and this was done . . . Then you get sufficient in the way of trust and commitment. And that engages people. . . .

Top managers in the public sector, where there are large numbers of professionals, have to be prepared to deal with scepticism. They have to stake their authority on the 'proof of the pudding'. If they set out their intentions and then deliver on them, however, professionals will decide that the managers are competent and morale improves. This can create a new and better attitudinal platform for strategic change.

FORMAL SYSTEMS

Formal systems for handling and negotiating change with employees have been based on consulting unions. It is a good idea to consult trade union representatives on planned strategic changes.

There may also be formal systems of involving all employees through service planning processes. These are based around an annual cycle of reviewing performance over the last 12 months and adjusting and setting goals for the next 12 months. This work is carried out by service managers and staff within operational units, but is normally approved only if it conforms to a framework set at the corporate and strategic level. In practice, the capacity of this process to engage employees with strategic vision is very variable. In some organisations the service planning process is carried out with genuine commitment and a high level of enthusiasm. In others the process is carried out in a perfunctory manner and little engagement is produced with corporate strategic change processes.

Finally, formal staff appraisal processes may be used as a management tool for achieving engagement with corporate-level strategic change processes. This process centres on what is normally an annual staff appraisal interview for each employee. This involves a review of the performance of individuals over the preceding 12 months by them and their boss, and agreement of the individual's objectives for the next 12 months. There may also be an element of planning the training and development of the individual. Monitoring interviews during the year may be used to follow up the annual interview.

The staff appraisal process can be linked to strategic visions and goals set at the corporate level. This may be attempted by linking the individual and corporate levels through service planning processes. So, the strategic goals of the organisation are used to set the goals of the operational units (for example, through annual service planning process). Then, individual objectives for each employee are based on the goals set in annual service plans. This means theoretically, and formally speaking, each individual is engaged with the strategic vision and strategic changes of the whole organisation. Many public sector organisations have introduced strategic goals, service planning, and staff appraisals. Many of these organisations have also striven to achieve high levels of alignment of individual efforts with strategic change in this way. Not surprisingly, in large organisations this can be a very complex process.

VALUING EMPLOYEES

Chief executives sometimes struggle with what they see as a major barrier to achieving high levels of engagement to strategic visions and strategic change. This barrier is the negative feelings that are believed to have built up over the many years of public sector reforms. These negative feelings are sometimes summed up in the idea that public sector employees feel undervalued or even not valued at all. Government attempts to change the public sector were sometimes accompanied by attacks on the reputation of professional employees. They were described as a pampered, indulged, secure, and unaccountable group of people. The public sector was seen as inefficient and bureaucratic, and thus professionals were accused of wasting the public's taxes. As a result, according to some senior managers in the public sector, professionals became cynical, mistrustful of managers brought in to sort out the professionals, resentful, and demoralised.

Professionals, in the mean time, have been expected to put up with a growing burden of accountability mechanisms, controls that constrain their discretion, reducing levels of pay and job security, declining unit costs, pressures to raise productivity, and demands for innovation.

The senior managers are mediators between the political pressures and the professionals. Some of them have a great deal of sympathy for the feelings of their staff. Others are more gung-ho about making changes despite the resentment and resistance of staff. All senior managers, however, have to deal with the problem of motivating staff and engaging them with the strategic vision and changes being sought. In consequence, some of the top managers in the public sector are concerned to demonstrate that their employees are valued. This can be attempted by taking the trouble to talk face to face to employees. This is about treating people with dignity and respect, feeling that they are entitled to explanations and information. This is difficult when there are issues and conflicts, but the aim is to show that management recognises the problems being experienced and values employees sufficiently to explain their actions and intentions. It is obviously much easier to meet employees when there is good news but more difficult when the anticipated reaction of employees is open hostility or pointed criticism of management performance. One of the hallmarks of a bureaucratic public sector organisation is that managers shirk the responsibility of face-to-face discussions with the people whom they manage (Crozier 1964).

Showing employees they are valued, however, goes beyond treating them with dignity by talking to them and providing explanations of management actions and intentions. In order to feel valued and appreciated by the organisation and managers, employees need to be rewarded for their efforts, skills, and performance. This can be done very powerfully through pay systems, but it can also be done through verbal and other recognition.

Some chief executives try to build a culture that values the efforts of all members of the organisation. This may be described sometimes as a team culture. While people may vary in their status and pay within the organisation, they seek to build the basic assumption that everybody is important and all make a vital contribution to the overall results achieved. They may try to do this through communication, training, or by simple personal example in how they interact with others.

Although there are some chief executives who speak and behave as if they have a low opinion of their employees and are intent on making changes despite them, making staff feel valued has emerged as one of the major issues for strategic change in many organisations. If staff feel valued, it is hoped, they will engage with the strategic vision and become champions of the changes that the chief executive and their management team are intent on making.

SUMMARY AND CONCLUSIONS

In this chapter we have looked at why top managers in the public sector want to engage employees and managers with long-term strategic visions and plans. Various rationales were considered. Some were negative such as the need to deal with resistance to change and overcome a lack of enthusiasm at lower levels of the organisation. Other rationales included a desire to unify the organisation and mobilise the organisation's most important resource—its employees. Issues of professionalism and conservatism were explored, as was the need for top management to secure a critical mass of support rather than total unanimity.

The nature of the process of engagement was investigated. It was concluded that engagement can be viewed as an intensive experience in which peoples' hearts and minds become linked to strategic changes. Less dramatically, engaging employees and managers can be seen as getting them interested and enthusiastic. Finally, it can be seen as what we might term a more mechanical phenomenon of ensuring that behaviour is aligned with corporate goals and plans.

The methods by which managers seek to achieve engagement were outlined. These included communication exercises, involvement processes, and formal systems. We also considered briefly the importance of valuing staff as a method of increasing engagement with strategic change.

No firm connections were suggested between different ideas of, and rationales for, engaging staff with strategic visions and plans and the methods used. It is possible, however, that there are connections. For example, those chief executives who appreciate the importance of staff being valued may be more likely than others to aspire to engaging the intellect and emotions of their employees to strategic change. Perhaps those who see engagement as a mechanical process of ensuring consistency between corporate-level goals and plans and individual behaviour are more likely to see the importance of setting up formal systems of annual service planning and staff appraisal. Then again, perhaps involvement schemes are favoured where top managers are concerned about a lack of enthusiasm lower down the organisation. Such connections certainly seem plausible, but in most public sector organisations there is usually a use of a range of methods in combination and the nature of engagement and its rationale are not seen in one-dimensional terms.

9
Focus and Align

INTRODUCTION

Even if public sector organisations did not have strategic planning processes, the fact that politicians with political objectives control the public sector would mean there was a recurrent need to focus and align budgets and activities. Elected politicians are elected for a set number of years and have things they want to accomplish in this time period. These things may well be defined within manifestos that are put before the electorate at the time of the election. They may legislate on them or make new policies. With each new crop of politicians in control, top managers have to set about changing the focus of the organisation and aligning activities to ensure the completion of the political objectives. The arrival of strategic management processes has only modified and not fundamentally altered this pattern. Political objectives (and legislative mandates) now inform strategic visions, goals, and plans, and the implementation of these again means there is a need to focus and align budgets and activities. Strategic-level activities, therefore, act as the bridge between political processes and the recurrent episodes of changes in budgets and activities.

Top managers trying to lead organisations and apply strategic management are quite conscious of this political framework. They may voice this as complaints about the short-term nature of elected politicians' concerns as a result of the election cycle.

The formal concern of strategic-level managers, however, is not the pressures coming down on them from elected politicians but how they are going to ensure that strategic visions and plans are made effective by reshaping budgets and activities. Further, they have concerns about changes to cultural and structural factors as ways of affecting budgets and activities. Although, sometimes, top public sector managers give the impression that changes in culture and structures are ends in themselves, rather than ways of affecting budgets and activities. Indeed, since much of any organisation's budget usually is spent on employing staff or purchasing services, it is arguably the case that changes in budget are also mainly an instrument for changes in activities. This can be boiled down to the idea that top managers want employees and contractors to know what they are supposed to be doing to implement the strategy and then doing what they are supposed to be doing. (We will concentrate on processes of focusing and aligning activities and budgets within the organisation; a later chapter looks at partnership working in which issues of co-ordination and co-alignment are important.)

This chapter begins by looking briefly at the causes of changes in the organisation. Then, the areas in which changes are made are considered. These include changes in resources, activities, culture, and structures. Then the processes that are used to make changes are examined. Several processes are outlined. These may be classified as processes of learning, communication and encouragement, controlling and managing, and quality management.

CAUSES OF CHANGE

Of course the main cause of any major change in a public sector organisation tends to be instigated by elected politicians. A chief executive in a local authority, which is closely overseen by elected politicians, will often explain that a specific change was made because the politicians wanted it. Naturally, the elected politicians will themselves be responding to events and trends. This can be seen reflected in the recent trend in the UK for politicians to conclude that there is a new set of public concerns that need addressing. These are sometimes referred to as the 'wicked issues' (environmental problems, economic regeneration, crime and disorder, etc.). They can be seen as the product of long-term trends in the economy, lifestyles and other social changes.

Top managers may be in a position to diagnose the need for changes alongside elected politicians. Some public organisations have experimented with forums in which elected politicians and top managers can discuss issues together and evaluate the need for new activities and new structures.

To the extent that public sector organisations have adopted strategic management processes, these political pressures and external trends and events are translated into strategic visions and strategic intent. These are then seen in managerial terms as the starting point for the management of change.

WHAT IS CHANGED?

When top managers in the public sector think about implementing strategic visions and strategic intent, they tend to think about changes in four aspects of their organisation:

- Resources
- Activities
- Culture
- Structures

Resources

Top managers have to think about and plan both capital and revenue expenditure. If a strategic goal is set that a major new service is going to be developed or extended in a significant way, the top managers will have to work out whether new buildings will be needed and how they will be financed. Then there will be revenue implications as well. The difficulties of making changes in this area are sometimes largely attributed to government decisions about public spending. This creates uncertainties about the occurrence of a revenue crisis that might, for example, cause problems in terms of the salaries of staff to work in the new service. This, of course, applies to public sector organisations where the government mainly determines the amount of income.

The problems caused by central government can be exaggerated. For a start, finance specialists advising top managers are able to guess and provide some foresight about government decisions. Moreover, many of the problems of using budgets for strategic purposes originate from internal problems. Overspends by some parts of the organisation cause drastic economising (or underspending) in other parts. Internal conflicts and empire building bedevil the rationality of annual budget-setting processes.

The key resources needed to implement strategic visions and plans are not just money. Increasingly top managers have defined people, skill, knowledge, and core competences as the resources that really make a difference in strategic terms. Some public sector chief executives now think of strategic service developments in terms of the people skills and specialist equipment needed. Assembling and sustaining the people with skills, and backing them up with the necessary technology and equipment are, for example, critical in the development of hospital services these days. Hospitals are nowadays making strategic decisions about which medical specialisations to try to hold on to and which to move into, and bound up in all of these decisions are calculations about resources and scarce skills.

Activities

Top managers in the public sector, unlike their stereotypical bureaucratic predecessors, are keen on having their organisations adopt new ways of doing things. Introducing new activities has become the hallmark of the new public sector manager. Changes in activities are a good thing. It is beneficial for the manager's career. Managers who can introduce new activities successfully are appreciated and complimented. They are seen as successful and they enhance their promotion prospects. The changes are also seen as good for the public because it is assumed that the new activities are delivering more value for money or saving money.

The general direction of changes in activities is towards more responsive and efficient services, both of which have been made political objectives by elected politicians who feel that these are popular with their electorates. So managers make strategic changes that deliver services more attuned to the needs of consumers of public services. At the same time top managers are consciously building performance management cultures, which means achieving planned results as efficiently as possible. In large public sector organisations top managers are trying to achieve changes in activities that reflect both of these goals. Their success tends to be uneven. Some parts of their organisations are more successful in these respects, and some parts may be poor. This then leads to a concern by managers about increasing the extent of responsiveness and efficiency across the board. They may formulate the need for changes in activities in terms of spreading best practice and achieving a critical mass of good quality and efficient services.

The time scale for across-the-board changes in the activities of a large complex organisation is sometimes reckoned to be 5 or 10 years. An experienced chief executive does not expect this to happen overnight.

Cultural change

Some top managers see changes in activities as flowing more or less automatically from cultural changes. There have been times when cultural change was seen as amenable to management action, providing there were enthusiastic and inspiring leaders. After many attempts in many different types of public sector organisation the early optimism has been tempered by experience. Top managers who aspire to change the culture of their organisation will now say that changes in culture are possible but cannot be achieved quickly and do require a lot of effort.

No doubt many senior managers in the public sector like to emphasise the uniqueness of their organisation and the distinctiveness of their organisation's culture. When it comes to fashioning a new culture for their own organisation, however, there is much similarity about the key components of the desired culture. One of these is that management and employees should act consistently to put the public first.

One implication of this cultural change may be seen as putting staff second. In this respect the new culture of public management clearly creates a tension for top management. Top managers now assert that employees are important. But years ago this was a taken-for-granted assumption in many public sector organisations that were producer-oriented and thus bureaucratic. Public sector reforms have challenged this producer orientation. For one thing more parts of the public sector are exposed to competition. Some chief executives and other senior managers began describing their organisations as 'businesses'. Of course, businesses also need to value their employees, but the growing use of the business metaphor and the increasing extent of competition were accompanied by a conviction that the public sector needed to be efficient in the use of resources and responsive to the needs of the public. On both accounts this implied a more critical evaluation of employee attitudes and behaviour.

This critical evaluation has been sharpest in relation to professional staff who may be seen as the most powerful producer interest group within the public sector. Top managers have at times made it clear that they could no longer make decisions primarily on the basis of the needs of professional employees. While this might create a more peaceful internal state of affairs for the managers, there is a danger that this will lead to decisions that put the organisation on a collision course with the political demands being made. In one way or another, to continue putting employees first could bring adverse consequences for the organisation.

The difficulty of this culture change can be illustrated in personal terms. A professional in, say, a government organisation, or a hospital, or a university may be placed at a senior level in the organisation's hierarchy. They may have entered public service after leaving university and have worked for 30 years in organisations that largely ran on bureaucratic lines. Their expectations for much of this time in public service would be that their career would consist of studying for professional qualifications, working to gain practical experience, observing professional norms of behaviour, and being rewarded by being promoted up the ladder. After years of faithfully pursuing this path professionals in a senior position believe that their qualifications and experience make them an expert on what the public needs are and how public service should be organised and delivered. The public sector reforms challenge these professional cultures—they may be expected to follow the orders of general managers without a background in their profession and told that the public should be consulted on what they need and how services can best be organised.

Top managers in the public sector may sympathise with the professional's attitude. They may believe that they must be patient and cannot change things all at once. Debates, persuasion, cajoling, and quiet diplomacy may be tried by the management of large public sector organisations. Implicitly, the managers are assuming that change has to be accomplished through an education process. They may think that the professional socialisation of people instils strong values and attitudes. Through education they hope these values and attitudes will change. The professionals have to be encouraged to change the way they think. They have to be convinced of the need to abandon old ideas of professionalism and develop a new partnership with the users of services and the beneficiaries of public sector activities. Key to this idea of partnership is that professionals should find out what the public wants and not assume they know best.

Professionals may resist this process of changing the culture. The chief executives and top managers often see them as an argumentative people. They expect tensions between management and professionals. The professionals may object to changes on the basis that they really do know better than the public. They have more advanced knowledge and in-depth experience than members of the public. In any case, it may be said, the public or the service user may have unrealistic expectations or may have dubious needs that the public service should not meet. For example, highly qualified hospital consultants may not feel the average member of the public understands enough to make sensible decisions about large-scale investment in medical technology. Teachers and lecturers may think it is foolish to ask students about how satisfied they are with their work loads and assessment requirements—surely students will want an easy life and standards will be lowered? Social workers protecting children at risk of abuse from their parents may suggest that it is inappropriate to accord the parents the status of customers.

Top managers encounter these counter-arguments and will admit that some of them are difficult issues for professionals. But they believe that if they keep on debating and arguing with the professionals, they will gradually win over more of them. And having won the intellectual argument, they believe that the practices of their organisation will change. Eventually, good practice—responsive and efficient public services—will be the norm and outdated professionalism will be an isolated phenomenon.

A second component of the new culture is that management and employees should internalise a value of continuous performance improvement. This is assumed to require that everybody in the organisation be committed to using performance indicators and performance measurement. This is often seen as a cultural phenomenon. As one chief executive put it: 'the existence of a prevailing culture which actually thinks about key performance indicators is very different. Baseline everything, change it, where you need to, so on, establish a new baseline, compare.'

Structural changes

The new public sector management that has emerged in recent years has not only introduced strategic management processes. It has also been quick to identify the need for structural changes as part of its agenda for strategic renewal and change. In many cases the top management have promoted both changes in the structure of the corporate centre and a radical departure from operational structures that have been in place over many years.

Chief executives in particular, who assume much of the responsibility for effective strategy implementation, have looked critically at the level and types of resources found in the corporate centre.

There has been increasing attention paid to the resources in the corporate centre for managing strategic planning and issue management. As chief executives have identified more and more strongly with a strategic leadership role, they have looked for more central support for this role. Strategic management specialists and units have been established with the aim of putting this support to the chief executive on a more professional basis. This has resulted in a much greater capability for providing strategic plans to central government departments or bodies set up by central government. It has also resulted in a central resource for co-ordinating corporate strategic plans and annual operational planning as part of an increased capacity for performance management.

In various parts of the public sector improvements in the corporate capacity and in corporate planning processes are evident. Universities plan and have set up teams or offices for carrying out the planning function. Local government has brought its service planning at the level of operational management into a framework of strategic corporate management systems and processes. Hospitals have long-term strategic plans and plans at unit level.

Not all of this development in strategic management capacity at corporate level is focused on financial planning and number crunching. In many organisations this corporate capacity is able to deliver issue management. In some cases, such as local government, the issue management capacity has been developed in response to a corporate agenda of community governance. The strategic issues being addressed are those of the community rather than of the organisation. Nevertheless, this has meant acquiring or developing skills within the corporate centre for partnership working and strategic management by a consortium of organisations.

Chief executives have also sometimes been dissatisfied with the resources in the corporate centre for dealing with press and media relationships and communications generally. This may reflect the special importance of public relations in the public sector. The public sector is meant to be more accountable and open than other sectors. It needs, therefore, a capability for communicating what it is doing, and explaining what it is doing. This is often done through the press and television rather than through direct means of communication to the public. There is a defensive element to this. The chief executive of a large public sector organisation will be keen to avoid actions by the organisation becoming a matter of embarrassment or controversy, and thus attracting unwelcome attention of politicians. On the positive side, this may also be linked to public sector reforms that are suggesting a need for all public sector organisations to address issues of concern to the public and to be more responsive to public needs. A more developed communication capability is useful in creating a dialogue with the public as part of a commitment to openness and responsiveness to the public. Among the other functions of an effective press and communications resource in the corporate centre is that of promoting a positive image of the organisation as efficient and innovative.

Many public sector organisations have operated over many years with quite a stable (some would say rigid) operating structure based on departments, directorates, and such like. At more or less the same time as strategic management has been introduced, public sector organisations have experimented with new structures at the level of operational management and service delivery. In some cases the idea has been to create decentralised structures that are more accountable for performance. In other cases, the aim has been to counter the fragmentation of 'departmentalism'. Chief executives have set corporate strategic goals and put pressure on departments to contribute to their achievement. They have been saying that they want a more corporate approach throughout the organisation, whereas a culture of 'departmentalism' encourages difficulties in inter-department working and an excessive concern for departmental priorities at the expense of the overall performance of the organisation. Departments have become empires led by department heads who want to pursue their own aims and minimise contact with corporate-level management.

Departmentalism has also been a problem because departmental managers have come into conflict with corporate-level management over the balance between strategic changes and maintaining current operations. Corporate managers have put pressure on operational managers to take a longer-term view and make strategic changes to achieve corporate goals. The operational managers have at times complained about the demands from the corporate centre, and suggested that they have a responsibility for maintaining services and activities and ensuring the organisation is meeting current needs of the service users. They have dragged their feet on making strategic changes and working towards corporate goals.

Chief executives, as the pivotal figure in strategic management, have been seeking to shift departments away from planning on a one-year time horizon (essentially an annual budget planning process) and towards a longer planning horizon. For long periods of time the operational level of management may pay lip-service to corporate strategic processes, and no major harm seems to result. But as one chief executive put it, top managers fear this approach makes the organisation as a whole vulnerable to external changes. His view was almost that of the classic critique of a bureaucratic public sector organisation (Crozier 1964). The organisation is used to doing what it does, is well trained in what it does, and sees no need to alter. If the chief executive is right, it seems likely that the organisation is doomed to periodic crises when it is forced to catch up with external realities. He would like the organisation to use strategic management to make the adjustment continuous and based on foresight.

Novel structural forms may be used to counter this departmentalism. For example, there have been experiments with executive managers who have a mix of corporate and departmental responsibilities. There has been a trial of rotating executive managers who look after a set of departments and then change to another set and so on; this was aimed at avoiding the empire building that occurs when a service or function has its own permanent head. Another is to break up the departmental structure of the organisation into a large number of smaller units, which presumably is designed to shift the balance of power between operational heads and the corporate centre. Another approach is to overlay hierarchical structures with project structures.

Structural changes have been given a lot of importance in the past. Some public sector managers seemed to equate strategic change with structural change. A more balanced view of structural change now seems to have emerged. Changes in organisational structure can help but there are other things that can and should be done as well.

Some chief executives in the public sector have consciously rejected pinning their hopes on structural change. They observe that many new chief executives put their mark on an organisation by quickly instigating restructuring. They have an assessment that the gains of making changes might be less than the costs of the disruption and the distraction caused by restructuring. Some top managers even say that structures do not matter. They say that it is the people that matter. If their hearts and minds are engaged with the strategic vision then the organisational structure is an irrelevancy to the effectiveness of strategic change. These managers want compelling evidence that the structure is dysfunctional before they would seriously consider restructuring.

MAKING CHANGES BY LEARNING

There are many organisations in the public sector, and they all move forward at different rates. Some stand out as leading edge organisations in their part of the public sector. This can be used by organisations wanting to make changes in activities, budgets, culture, or structure in order to align them with their strategy. They can study the leading edge organisations, copying what works and avoiding the mistakes that being the first often entails. This approach of learning from the best seems to offer the chance to manage strategic change effectively, without suffering from the setbacks that are part and parcel of experimentation. The implication is of course that the organisation always trails just behind the leading edge organisations.

In large organisations it is also possible to make changes by piloting them in one part of the organisation, establishing the right way to make changes, and then 'rolling out' the change throughout the rest of the organisation. This approach, which involves disseminating the best ways of making changes, resembles the previous one. In this case, however, the leading edge of change is deliberately created within the organisation to allow management to learn from experimentation.

Learning of a different kind plays a part in some attempts to change corporate cultures. Chief executives may plan to change culture by picking out instances of best practice within their organisation because they are exemplars of the culture they wish to reinforce. By publicising and disseminating knowledge of these best practices through management seminars and presentations, they hope that others will absorb the culture and then go on to produce their own best practice. For example, one unit of an organisation may do some good work on improving customer care and this will then be picked up by top management and celebrated for others to learn from.

In this process the managers are using exemplars to promote messages about the kind of organisation it is and the sorts of practices that receive praise and recognition. This may start off as a trickle of exemplars, but it is hoped that dissemination will build up the numbers of examples, and finally that it will add up to a stream that may be labelled as a strategic change based on a new culture.

Learning can be important in yet another way in bringing about changes. Sometimes public sector organisations have become so bureaucratic that decision making in the ordinary way becomes difficult. Managers find it difficult to discuss face to face with their employees what changes are to be made, and employees stick rigidly to their current job descriptions and customary practices. In these circumstances, some public sector organisations have found it useful to tackle the management of change through training and staff development events. It is as though important decisions can only be made by getting people to talk face to face in situations where the usual rules and management hierarchy are suspended. So, by labelling the situation as a training or learning one there can be innovation and renewal, whereas in the normal work situation people are locked into a bureaucratic state of immobility. The development of corporate strategies by public sector organisations in events designed according to the principles of 'whole systems development' could be seen as an example of how learning situations can be used to break out of bureaucratic impasses. One study of the use of whole systems development by the public sector stressed how important it was that top management was seen to learn in public in the presence of 280 employees and service users (Wilkinson & Pedler 1996). This could be seen as evidence that very bureaucratic organisations find it difficult to make changes through their ordinary management systems and need overtly 'learning' events to make decisions.

COMMUNICATIONS AND ENCOURAGEMENT

Some managers try to make changes without giving orders and commands. Instead they use communications to bring about change. This may be referred to as communicating 'messages' and sending 'signals' to managers and employees at lower levels. There is an assumption in this behaviour that managers and employees at operational levels are responsive to the wishes of top management. One chief executive sees it as a compliment to top managers if people at lower levels in the organisation attempt to solve problems by considering how the top managers would tackle them. In such an organisation, messages from above help those lower down to know the approaches to problems favoured by those at the top. Signals may confirm the seriousness of messages. This use of communications to bring about change has the virtue of leaving the actual decision making in the hands of those who know the operational realities while ensuring that it is consistent with corporate intentions. In the best possible scenario, the use of communications to influence decision making brings about change that reflects both the official strategic plans of top managers and operational realities.

This does not work in all public sector organisations. Some top managers know that messages will be rejected by people lower down the hierarchy as propaganda. Even where those lower down are not suspicious of the messages being sent, top managers have to think carefully how they formulate and saturate the organisation with messages. Judgements have to be made about the optimum number of messages to send out, the simplicity or complexity of the messages, how they can be reinforced, and how they can be changed. Part of the judgement is about how to avoid the messages appearing to be propaganda, and what communication vehicles are best for this purpose.

It may be useful to distinguish messages from signals. Messages may be communicated in verbal or written form and may be transparent in meaning. For example, the chief executive may make speeches saying how important it is for the organisation to become more responsive to the public's needs. It might be argued that signals are communicated via actions or decisions and their meaning is perceived by managers and employees in the context of statements made by top managers. The decisions to upgrade complaint procedures and provide reception staffs with customer care training may be seen as signals that the organisation is serious about becoming customer focused. An increasing tendency for top managers to meet with front-line employees may signal that the organisation values the views of its ordinary employees. There may also be signals that undermine messages communicated by top managers.

Public sector managers have put out many messages in recent years. For example, there has been a message that creativity and innovation are valued. Chief executives have tried to make it clear that they would welcome managers and employees who try to do things differently and do not just carry on doing the things they have always done. The message has often gone out that service managers and employees should be imaginative and take risks—that they will not be blamed if some things they try do not work. The message has certainly gone out that top management wants managers to use their initiative. The message has also been repeated endlessly in a whole range of organisations that front-line people should listen to what the public wants and then apply what they have learnt to improving the organisation.

Some chief executives have espoused management by encouragement as superior to central dictate. It is felt that orders from the centre will constrain innovation and creativity. They may see the capacity for change as dependent not on the centre—which provides a general pressure for change—but on the initiative of individuals at lower levels of the organisation. The encouragement from the corporate centre has several elements. It encourages the individuals to:

• Have confidence in their ability to innovate
• Persist in the face of bureaucratic difficulties
• Use their discretion in the use of devolved budgets

This encouragement backs up the message that the corporate centre wants individuals to have good ideas. Rewarding the individuals who succeed in trying out new ideas signals support for this message. The message is reinforced by public appreciation of local initiatives and recognition through celebration of successes in management forums.

This approach cannot encourage or reward any and every use of local initiative. The public sector is answerable to elected politicians, so there needs to be an approximate correspondence between what the politicians want to happen and the initiatives being taken by managers and employees at lower levels. Providing this is the case, top managers can feel that it is not necessary for them to produce all change through the implementation of very centralised decisions. In other words, they do not need detailed control of all the changes that are made. Indeed, they may feel that they are so remote from where the changes are made that they would be more than likely to make dysfunctional decisions.

This process of making changes by encouragement seems to require as much as four building blocks to work. First, there needs to be a level of communication so that top managers can feel confident that the strategic vision and corporate values are well understood and enjoy a reasonable level of commitment from people in the organisation. Second, top managers have to feel confident that they have succeeded to some degree in convincing many people in the organisation that there is a unity of purpose and that everybody is contributing to a team effort. Third, the top managers have to feel that praise is a fairly potent method of rewarding individuals who have tried to change things and do new things. Finally, the top managers need to be able to reward successful initiatives by individuals through pay or promotions. If these building blocks do not exist, it is unlikely that top managers are going to feel able to rely on encouragement to make changes.

CONTROLLING AND MANAGING CHANGE

Some managers rely on management systems to make changes. Performance management systems are possibly the most common way of achieving focus and alignment. Typically they provide for the setting of performance goals on the basis of the organisation—strategic goals or aims. These performance goals are set for service units but may be used to align individual or team behaviour through annual performance appraisal systems.

In recent years there has also been the option of using the European Foundation for Quality Management (EFQM) excellence model, which provides a tool for analysing how to make changes in leadership, policy and strategy, people management, resources, and processes to achieve changes in organisational results. This is primarily seen by top managers as a self-assessment framework for managers with the added advantage that it features customer satisfaction as a key result area.

If an organisation decides to go down the self-assessment route then they will have to train assessors and evidence will have to be collected (e.g. customer satisfaction). One of the results of such a process is to make managers more aware of how their organisation works and what outcomes they should be measuring. Another result is to make the satisfaction of the customer (service user) more important for the manager. In many cases it causes services to develop arrangements for knowing what service users think of the organisation and its services.

One chief executive in an organisation that was preparing to use the self-assessment model was very impressed by the way it had caused his managers to think more about what they were doing. He mentioned, in particular, the way that it had brought out into the open some strange ideas about the identity of the service users. Reflecting on this experience, he said that it could not be assumed that managers had analysed who used their services.

Another way of managing and controlling changes is to check on the alignment of services with strategy through periodic management reviews. In UK local government experiments in bringing in a duty of best value led to the setting up of formal reviews that require managers to go through all the organisation's activities. There is even the possibility in this system of reviews of services to involve elected politicians who can be expected to have strong regard for the alignment of the service with their political objectives. These reviews could also provide elected politicians with the detailed insights they need to challenge service providers on the basis of the alignment of the service with efforts at community problem solving.

For organisations that put a lot of emphasis on aligning values and culture with the strategic changes that are being made, a system of reviews of service plans or team plans can be used to check on the adoption of values throughout the organisation. For example, many organisations have written statements of core values (e.g. putting services to the public first, equal opportunities, valuing employees, taking action to be more efficient and effective, aiming for quality, caring for the environment). As part of the reviews of plans top managers can ask those responsible what they had done over the preceding period to put services to the public first and how this value is enacted within the current plan.

Resource allocation systems may be used to great effect. One way of making sure that activities are realigned to implement strategic visions and plans is to make resource allocations conditional on appropriate resource requests and on past performance. Bushnell & Halus (1992) make the point about resource requests in their review of strategic planning in the public sector: 'One of the most powerful tools to elicit acceptance is to closely link resource allocation with the priorities and strategies in the plan. Those parts of an agency that do not justify their resource requirements in terms of the plan are likely to be denied the resources they feel they need' (p. 366). Even tougher is making resource allocations on the basis of a comparison of last year's actual performance against performance targets derived from strategic goals.

For these management systems to be effective there has to be a judicious willingness on the part of management to use them to take tough decisions and see them through. There may be just one or two major decisions that must be taken on this basis in a three- or four-year period, but management may have to be prepared to be unpopular for a time and determined to stand by the decisions taken. This is most acute in cases where alignment of activities or resources with new strategies calls for the ending of activities. This may even involve closing operational units. This may arise, for example, where public needs have changed and resources have to be switched to adjust the organisation to the new realities. This has happened on a large scale throughout the public sector. Health services have put more resources into primary care and closed older hospitals. Education has had to close some schools and open others as demographic changes have affected the need for schools at different levels of the education system. Universities have closed down some departments and opened new ones as the industrial and economic system has been reshaped by technological and economic changes. Local government is always losing statutory responsibilities and gaining new ones.

QUALITY AND STRATEGIC MANAGEMENT

Quality management has also been used to bring about changes in activities. This can be organised on TQM principles and use bottom-up approaches to improving activities. It is often supported by training and development of employees (e.g. customer awareness training).

Of most relevance here are ideas of using quality management in conjunction with strategic planning. Bushnell & Halus (1992) refer to a case that suggests that such a combination is powerful in renewing ailing public sector organisations. The US Coastguard Yard in Curtis Bay, Maryland was almost shut down because of rising costs and competition from private shipyards. Bushnell & Halus (1992, p. 355) report that 'three years after beginning a series of top management meetings and strategic planning sessions, its commanding officer, Captain Robert Yuhas, feels confident that it can now compete with any shipyard. The turnaround, he contends, can be in large part credited to the collaborative development and careful implementation of a strategic plan orchestrated within a total quality management (TQM) framework.'

Total quality management in practice within the public sector is not easily encapsulated. Is it a philosophy or a strategy? Is it used comprehensively or piecemeal? In the United States public sector it began in the late 1980s and continued through the 1990s. One study of city governments in the USA found that, in practice, quality management activities typically involved monitoring customer satisfaction and, less commonly, benchmarking (Berman 1998). Only a minority (1 in 10) of cities had 'a commitment to a broad range of TQM activities in 1993' (Berman 1998, p. 156).

At its most comprehensive TQM can involve 'customer orientation, reengineering, continuous improvement, empowerment, and benchmarking' (Berman 1998, p. 157). It is evident, therefore, that old-style strategic planning can be enriched with features of TQM in various ways. For example, mission statements, goals, and performance targets can be based on outcomes for the public. The setting of strategic goals and performance goals can be predicated on the basis of continuous improvement. Re-engineering can be used to support units achieve performance goals based on strategic planning. Lower-level managers and employees can be empowered through the appropriate design of strategic planning processes. For example, events and meetings can be used to include employees in developing strategic plans. Benchmarking can be used to set performance targets. It can also be used, as Holloway and her fellow researchers suggest, for process improvements in areas critical for the strategic plan. 'In theory, best practice benchmarking helps organisations to improve strategically important processes' (Holloway et al. 1999, p. 6).

SUMMARY AND CONCLUSIONS

In this chapter we have noted the interlinked reasons for changing activities, resources, culture, and organisational structures. These were recurrent changes in political objectives, reflecting changed external conditions, and leading to changes in strategic vision and strategies.

The nature of changes to focus and align the organisation in the light of the need to implement new strategic visions and strategies was considered. The problems of budgeting processes and other kinds of resources were examined. Then there was a look at changes in activities and the attempts there have been to bring about across-the-board changes in activities. Cultural changes were explored mainly in relation to responsiveness to the public and performance management to achieve efficiency. Finally, changes in the nature of the corporate centre and operational management were looked at under the heading of organisational changes.

A comprehensive look at making changes was approached in terms of learning, communications and encouragement, and management systems. The role of learning in making changes was examined from a number of angles, including learning from leading edge organisations, learning from pilots, and learning situations as a way of creating innovation in bureaucratic settings. Communications and encouragement were generally considered from the point of view of fostering changes made at the initiative of managers and employees at lower levels. The use of messages and signals was briefly outlined, and the nature and building blocks of managing

change by encouragement were discussed. The idea of using management systems to manage and control changes was presented. The
management systems considered included performance management, service reviews, and reviews of service and team planning to
check on the adoption of values. The need for tough decisions to
enforce realignments was noted—especially in cases where activities
needed to be ended.

Finally, the benefits of using quality management in conjunction
with strategic management were explored.

10

Stabilising and Ensuring Targets are Achieved

INTRODUCTION

The importance of making change happen in the public sector is now widely recognised in management circles. But less recognised is the importance of making sure that strategic changes are finished off and that a change does not get stuck partway through. This requires that managers consolidate changes—stabilise them—and check that strategic targets have been accomplished. If these things are not done then the planned provision of improved and new benefits for the public will not be achieved or will produce only disappointing results.

The methods of stabilising changes and checking that targets are achieved are relatively familiar. They involve planning and performance management activities and rewarding employees. Wilkinson & Monkhouse (1994) have questioned the effectiveness of monitoring systems in the public sector: 'It is reasonable to assume that an organization will measure those aspects that are deemed to be important within it; most people would think so but the reality is often quite different within the public sector' (p. 18). Bushnell & Halus (1992) suggest that information on output or performance measures is often lacking. This would certainly make it difficult for a public sector organisation to know whether a strategic change has been successful. The relationship between individual performance and rewards is also often less close than might be considered desirable. Current weaknesses in these basics of the management of change may be put down to the tradition of bureaucratic stability and order. New managers are trying to make a break with this tradition and are acting on the basis of values of innovation and change. But weaknesses in performance management exist and more attention must be paid to processes that demonstrate empirically that the public is better served by the changes being made.

In this chapter the purpose of stabilising change and ensuring targets are achieved will be considered, as well as some of the nuances of these activities. The methods of stabilising change and ensuring targets are achieved will be examined in detail.

THE POLITICAL PRESSURE TO DELIVER RESULTS

Corporate strategic plans are meant to be the blueprints for strategic changes. They should also identify what the organisation is trying to achieve—the strategic targets. If the strategic planning process has worked as it should have done, these targets will not be merely formulated by managers and possibly other members of the organisation and the public, they will also reflect the political objectives and priorities of elected politicians. Consequently, ensuring that strategic changes are consolidated and ensuring that strategic targets are achieved matters from the point of view of the effectiveness of representative democracy. Moreover, top managers who fail to ensure that they are achieving the things that the elected politicians want are risking losing political support, and may soon find their positions very uncomfortable.

MANAGEMENT CAPACITY

Management problem-solving resources have to be invested wisely if the organisation is not to become overextended. Organisations that are fast growing or changing rapidly are vulnerable to exceeding the limits of their management capacity. Growth and change both create a need for managers to solve problems. If too much growth or change is launched the unsolved problems accumulate rapidly and the organisation finds itself in a crisis. Wise investment of management resources means optimising rather than maximising management time allocated to starting off innovations. In other words, an organisation must make sure that management time is put into stabilising changes and monitoring strategic targets as well as starting off innovations. This means, of course, that investment of management time in non-priority areas is forgone as a luxury the organisation cannot currently afford. Therefore, allocating management capacity for stabilising change and ensuring targets are being achieved is important in order to deliver on the important priorities.

Obviously the strategic plan determines what is and what is not a priority area, and thus should constrain how management time is allocated. This is really yet another argument about the importance of the organisation being focused when it makes strategic changes. In this case, the argument is that the limited amount of management capacity requires that there be focused action to achieve strategic targets.

WHAT IS THE PROCESS OF STABILISING CHANGE AND ENSURING TARGETS ARE ACHIEVED?

What is stabilising change? First, it is about top management trying to mesh together the priorities and objectives of the politicians and the bottom-up interests and commitment of managers and employees. There may be changes that have to be made to the top priority because this is the wish of politicians. But operating units may not be keen on them or may have also identified changes that they would like to see happen. Strategic development is more likely where strategic changes are planned so as to reconcile top-down and bottom-up pressures. It is also possible to achieve some reconciliation through the process of making the changes. For example, if a consultation approach is used it may be possible for service managers and employees to obtain adjustments to the changes so that there is a closer match to their own interests. Or, reward systems may be used to provide the extrinsic motivation to ensure the changes are maintained. If reconciliation is not possible, or fails, then the change may quickly run into the ground. There needs to be support for seeing changes through to a successful conclusion.

Stabilising change is in part about taking measures to prevent strategic changes fading away. One fear is that if management fails to set milestones and clear performance targets and then fails to ensure a system of monitoring, changes will be made for a while and then gradually and quietly dropped. This may reflect an asymmetry in management attention—a high level of attention when a change is made, and no attention when it is dropped. How many innovations have been introduced with a fanfare of trumpets and a blaze of glory, only to be allowed to fade away shortly afterwards?

Ensuring targets are achieved requires that milestones along the way are set. These may not be easy to fix. Top managers make judgements about the rate at which change can be made and how much innovation can actually be accomplished. There may be disagreements among the top management team about how long it will take to achieve the strategic targets. Some will be pessimistic and suggest that change will be achieved only with difficulty and very slowly. Others will argue for quicker change. This can lead to quite protracted debates among management. These should not be left as theoretical or abstract debates. The empirical results of the changes need to be assessed systematically and regularly. If there are disagreements among managers about how much can be achieved then it is very important that milestones of achievement are clear, otherwise change can become bogged down without anybody being ready to intervene and get the change back on track.

Ensuring targets are achieved also means stopping changes and innovations. Changes may be promoted by different parts of the organisation. An organisation may try to do too many different things. This can be disruptive for the achievement of strategic targets. It can be dysfunctional in terms of the competition for limited management time and investment funding. The top management needs at times, therefore, to block changes in order to ensure that the top priority changes can be pursued and that they have adequate resources. They may have to say to parts of the organisation that the changes they are promoting will have to wait their turn.

USING CONTROL TO STABILISE CHANGES AND ACHIEVE TARGETS

Individual public sector organisations that have launched major long-term strategic change programmes may introduce or enhance performance management systems to ensure change is stabilised. Top managers have to rely on performance management systems to make sure that change projects are working. This involves planning the performance expected on the basis of the changes, picking performance indicators, setting actual targets, and top managers carrying out monitoring based on reports. Performance management systems for operating units can be underpinned by individual staff appraisal interviews. Both are based on the idea that control is achievable through setting performance targets and measuring performance. The objectives set for individuals can be chosen to help with achieving performance targets of operating units.

Some organisations now have plans and monitoring frameworks for all their main strategic programme areas. The monitoring frameworks are designed to show management teams, governing boards, and elected politicians how well the organisation is doing. If the change process has been set up properly, then the continued effectiveness of innovations can be checked using formal reports containing data on performance indicators.

The control offered by performance management systems, to repeat, is just as important to maintain change as it is to apply pressure for increased efficiency. Obviously, therefore, the issue is not just having a performance management system but using it for the express purpose to aid management efforts to make strategic changes. This means that the detail of how the performance management system is used is important. For example, the selection of performance indicators and targets for regular reporting will affect how easy it is to use the performance management system to monitor the consequences and impact of specific strategic changes. Public organisations that are innovative often find it difficult to use existing reporting systems to show that individual innovations have worked. The processes of making changes and reporting performance information are evidently out of alignment. This could either mean that the current performance indicators do not have any clear link to the strategic vision and strategic goals of the organisation, or that the changes being made do not have much relevance to strategic plans. Either the reporting system's performance indicators need to be changed or the organisation should review its process for prioritising what changes to make.

If the performance indicators need to be changed, then the organisation will need to begin with the strategy and translate this into specific performance goals and targets. There may need to be further changes to the performance management system. For example, information systems may need to be improved.

There is in the end no alternative but for top managers to set up arrangements for monitoring the results of change and then spending time doing just that—that is, monitoring results. They then have to concentrate particularly on those areas of the organisation that are not reaching the performance targets. This includes the case of areas where there has been change and the outcomes have been less than expected. Therefore, top managers have to be able and willing to confront performance gaps.

The level of intervention by top managers in the face of problems revealed by reports obviously depends on how bad the performance is. Exceptionally bad performance requires quick and firm action by top managers. Plans will not work on the basis of their technical excellence alone. Plans have to be monitored and then backed by the use of power. If they are not, then the changes made falter or can disintegrate.

The way in which public sector organisations approach the planning process—for example, by often involving operational managers in the formulation of operational goals and plans—influences the character of the monitoring. An organisation's top management may define the overall mission and strategic objectives. Operating units are then asked to assess their environment and identify issues, as well as make proposals for developing operational activities. These assessments, analyses, and proposals may be presented within service or business plans (the terminology varies). The corporate level of the organisation then puts these together to see what this means for the overall strategic development of the organisation. The top managers may then require changes in the operational plans in the light of their consideration of priorities, strategic goals, and resources. The corporate centre obviously has some choice in how prescriptive it is and to what extent it attempts to modify and adjust operational planning by units. How all this is handled must have some influence on how centralised the organisation feels and how controlling the top managers are.

REWARDS

Rewards can be seen as an alternative to controls to ensure changes are maintained and targets achieved. Whereas controls are based on the idea that top management must act to impose these things, rewards are used on the assumption that others can be given incentives that make them want to maintain changes and achieve targets. In practice, managers may use a combination of controls and rewards.

There is a range of incentives being used in the public sector. Some are aimed at the unit and some are aimed at individuals. One approach is to use praise and recognition to reward managers and employees who have achieved and sustained successful changes. Praise and recognition can also be used to motivate management development and focus and align organisational activities, and may be carried out in very public ways. Top managers sometimes doubt the power of such a method of rewarding desired behaviour. It remains, however, one of the methods used.

Some top managers feel that personally expressed appreciation is motivating. For example, one chief executive has a practice of sending a note to individuals in respect of specific achievements. He also makes an effort to let people know that he thinks they are doing a good job.

A second approach to incentives is to link future investment in a unit to how well a change is implemented and targets are met. This may be done using a special investment fund and setting appropriate criteria for a competitive bidding process.

Financial reward for individuals is a third method. Some organisations have brought in bonuses and performance-related pay. These tend to cover top and middle managers. The sums of money involved may not always be that large, but then some managers believe that their importance is symbolic. The system may be based on an appraisal process, and involve target setting for individuals, and annual performance reviews. Performance-targeting and review processes also seek to make performance expectations clear for individuals. So, rewards–expectations ratios are at the core of this approach to providing incentives. They can be controversial in the public sector, but this may be just the early phase when they are being implemented. One chief executive said that after operating for five or six years financial rewards for individuals had ceased to be controversial. People had become used to it.

One complication arises where performance-related pay is part of a review process that is also intended to drive a personal development process. There has been a presumption over many years that these different functions are hard to reconcile through a single appraisal interview.

SUMMARY AND CONCLUSIONS

The issues of stabilising change and ensuring targets are achieved have been linked to the need to ensure that politicians' priorities and objectives are met and to the need to focus action in the light of limited management capacity.

The processes of stabilising change and ensuring targets are achieved were reviewed. They were seen to involve top management meshing together the priorities and objectives of the politicians and the interests and commitment of managers and employees. They were seen to involve top managers taking measures to prevent strategic changes fading away. Then there is the importance of setting milestones so that achievements are clear, and action can be taken to keep change on track. Finally, it was noted that ensuring targets are achieved also means stopping changes and innovations.

The approaches to stabilising change and ensuring targets are achieved have been mainly considered to comprise a control-based or a reward-based approach. In particular, the design and operation of performance management and different types of rewards were outlined.

Thus, performance management and reward systems are critical to the success management has in sustaining successful strategic changes and achieving performance targets. The basic principles of these systems may seem simple enough, but this may be a deceptive simplicity. Experienced and very successful chief executives say that it is important to put in good systems. They also say that putting them in and making them effective is hard work.

It is striking that the key to successful change is really about institutionalising new activities within the organisational framework. It might be said that successful changes comprise moving to a new 'equilibrium'. In this sense, installing and using performance management and reward systems to secure change imply a paradox in public sector management. This may be summarised as follows. Successful managers are agents of strategic changes and improved services to the public. They are keen to challenge and undermine existing bureaucratic practices. But then they work in order to develop 'rigidity' about new activities. This means that it is not enough to be creative and imaginative and see what are only abstract possibilities in the current situation. Change also requires managers who can work with persistence and discipline to turn the abstract ideas into empirical results. It takes a lot of hard work using performance management and reward systems. Some public sector organisations are trying to cultivate the qualities of persistence, discipline, and hard work in their managers to round them out and complement their current taste for generating imaginative ideas and the intellectual challenge of visioning new services.

11

Involving the Public

INTRODUCTION

Bureaucratic public sector organisations have become the objects of much criticism (Osborne & Gaebler 1992). The hallmarks of bureaucratic public sector organisations are not just red tape and rigidity created by slavish adherence to rules. They also include a lack of communication with the public and an ethos of serving the interests of the bureaucrat rather than the users of services.

In this chapter we look at the different ways in which top managers in the public sector are seeking to involve the public in strategic changes and thus create more responsive public sector organisations. They may use consultation as a method of involvement to find out what the public thinks or wants prior to, during, or after changes. They may design involvement techniques to improve the knowledge used to design services. They may use involvement as a way of sharing decision making with the public. They may be aiming at building the public's sense of involvement and identification with the public sector. Involving the public is a diverse phenomenon.

The use of organisational changes, specific techniques, and cultural changes are examined. Before looking at these, the motives and the nature of involvement activity are described.

THE POLITICAL AGENDA

One reason why public sector managers are trying to find ways to consult and involve the public is simply that some elected politicians have identified this as important. Politicians began pressing for this very strongly in the 1990s. In the United States the Government Performance and Results Act of 1993 required federal agencies to develop strategic plans. When developing their plans the federal agencies were required to consult with those who were affected by or interested in their strategic plan. In other words, federal agencies were required to incorporate stakeholder inputs into their strategic plan. These stakeholders included the federal agencies' customers.

In the United Kingdom politicians have made consulting the public a legal duty for local government in the context of a policy known as 'best value'. Achieving the involvement of the public is seen as challenging and problematic, but national government has succeeded in convincing top managers that they should take it seriously. The emphasis is on involving service users in decisions about service delivery.

Managers may feel that pursuit of user involvement is a good thing to do in principle, but politicians can use legislation and encouragement to ensure that the challenge of user involvement is confronted and made a high priority.

This political pressure to consult and involve the public seems to be associated with a change of perspective about the nature of public sector activity. Some years ago too many public sector managers and workers were isolated from the public that they were there to serve. The isolation of the services from the public was captured in a joke told by a top manager. 'I once cracked a joke, that if somebody had removed the 40 000 council houses that I was working with at the time, then the housing department would still have run for at least a good two or three years, because they wouldn't have noticed that they weren't there.' Isolated from the public, many had become rather indifferent to the needs of the public they were meant to serve. University lecturers would joke that universities would be all right if there were no students! Other professional groups made similar jokes about their clients. Indifference was reinforced in some cases by a feeling of superiority over the public. Reception staff would refer contemptuously to the public as 'punters'. Some individuals could be aggressive and hostile to their clients and service users, as shown by occasional service user complaints of employee rudeness.

The political imperative to involve the public is linked to more managers now seeing service users as important people to please and satisfy. In some cases managers are seeing service users as partners and co-operators. 'We no longer just deliver services at people. We do [service delivery] with them and for them and I think that change is now firmly ingrained, even in services which are statutory ones.' In this sense, the public sector is moving towards a partnership with the public, and its former paternalism is fading.

Some of the motivation for politicians to put pressure on public sector managers to consult and involve service users is that many politicians have become concerned about the vitality and robustness of representative democracy. Getting public sector managers to involve the public in decisions on service delivery is just one of a number of initiatives in Britain that are aiming at democratic renewal. There are involvement initiatives aimed at young people in particular, a group that are important for the future of active citizenship and representative politics.

INVOLVEMENT AS EDUCATION

Quite another motive for involving the public is the idea that through involvement the public can be educated. Different managers have different views on this education through involvement.

Ever since the new right politicians came to power in the 1970s and 1980s the public sector has been living with the threat of budget cuts and retrenchment. The modernisers of the public sector in the 1990s called on public sector managers to do more with less. So there have been years and years of public sector managers contemplating possible gaps between their resources and the level of demand for public services. This leads directly to one of the reasons why top managers can see some advantage in involving the public. They hope that through involvement the public will see that resources are limited and will then be educated into a realistic set of expectations about service delivery. In the course of involvement there are opportunities for dialogue between the public sector organisation and the service users. The public sector organisation is educated about the needs of the service user, and the service user educated about the capabilities of the organisation.

For some managers the aim of this education through involvement is a satisfied public. Without education, they think, the public has unrealistically high expectations and service delivery is a disappointment. With education, the public has a realistic set of expectations and service delivery matches these expectations. Where there is a match between expectations and service delivery, then public satisfaction is the logical result.

Some managers also think that involvement can also be useful in educating the public to understand and accept changes made by the public sector managers. In the process of involvement managers can explain to service users what the choices were and why one option was chosen rather than another. Also, changes can leave some members of the public winners and some losers. Through involvement some managers hope that they can convince those losing out that the net benefits of the change justify the changes. The logic of such a rationale for involvement may sound idealistic. But in managing change some public sector managers feel that it is best to inform people sooner rather than later about a decision they will not like and explain the grounds for the decision. If this is done, it is suggested that people are more likely to understand the decision.

Another argument for involvement of the public concerns the problem of citizens who resent paying for services that they do not actually use. Some public services that receive large sums of public money have relatively small numbers of direct beneficiaries. In a period in which there has been a challenge to the need for a large public sector, and pressure to reduce the tax burden due to public services, the providers of services may become concerned about the attitudes of non-users of their services. Therefore, managers may hope that higher levels of public involvement may produce a more sympathetic attitude among non-users of particular services. (Another option is to focus public relations campaigns on services that are widely used and popular in order to remind people that they benefit from collective provision even if they do not use all the services that are provided through the public sector.)

A final reason for favouring involvement as a way of educating the public is that an organisation wants to counter hostile press reports. For example, local authorities in Britain often suffer from what they regard as unfair and negative press reports. By having a high level of public involvement, public sector managers may hope to use the involvement channels to present a different perspective. Furthermore, the existence of a high level of public involvement may provide useful data with which public sector managers can counter inaccurate press reports on the state of public feeling.

IMPROVING SERVICES

Involving the public can educate public sector professionals as well as the public. This is especially the case if it is the professionals that take part in the involvement process. When professionals consult service users and ask them about the service they can learn some surprising things. Probably most importantly, service users may alert professionals to quite different priorities among members of the public. This applies to regulatory services as well as other non-marketed services. If the professionals listen to what the public tells them and they change what they do and how resources are allocated, then public involvement has re-educated the professionals. There are many cases where professionals have chosen to consult and involve the public, and have made changes in their activities as a result, showing that professionals are capable of playing a leading role in the development of more responsive public services.

However, politicians and top managers have been at the forefront of pointing out that there is much to be gained by involving the public in improving the services. The public has information on the services. They have ideas that managers can exploit. But, critically, better government may be defined in part as the public sector better meeting the needs of the public. And who knows better than the public what their needs are? One chief executive suggested that, 'an effective organisation would obviously be open to the views of the people it exists to serve and to some extent hopefully occasionally please'. He was convinced that the public 'could help us do things better'. He defined doing things better as 'doing things in a way which better meets their needs, better meets their aspirations, more affordably, more economically'.

In the absence of help from the public, the public sector can be far from perfect in how it operates. Common complaints by service users are being kept waiting in hospital waiting rooms, slow or unjust treatment of applications, poor administration of benefits and grant payments, poor quality work, poor teaching in schools, discriminatory behaviour against ethnic minorities by police forces, and so on. Many managers are admitting that in the past the public has been poorly served. Many would also admit that the public sector was too often putting the interests and convenience of service providers before that of service users. This is attributed in part to the fact that the members of the public who were receiving services did not have any say. The power to make decisions rested largely with the bureaucrats.

Involving the public can be of direct use in checking on the performance of the public sector. Many organisations in the public sector have begun monitoring the level of public satisfaction with services. They may want to check out systematically just how good the services are and to make sure that they are not deluding themselves about the quality of the services. Large-scale surveys may be commissioned to provide baseline data and then follow up surveys may be used to check on the success of changes made by organisations.

Managers may want more than simple satisfaction surveys. Large stratified samples can be used to investigate what the members of the public think they want, and how well they think services actually meet their needs.

Surveys are only one way of deepening the involvement of the public. They are mainly useful for obtaining information. Public and user involvement will need developing further if it is going to help with the identification of current needs of the public either as communities or as users of specific services. If the public sector is going to make good use of strategic management for planning for the long term, it will need to make use of consultation and involvement to look at the needs of future generations. Strategic management is concerned with the future, and so the managers of the public services need to be thinking about 10 or 20 years ahead. What will users of health services in the future need? What will the students of the future need from schools and universities? What will the clients of welfare services need? Moreover, what are the implications of these future needs not only for the content of services but also for the service delivery interface with the public? For instance, will information and communication technology be a key to the way in which the public obtains access to services and provides information to governments?

THE DEMOCRACY ARGUMENT

Involving the public in service delivery decisions may be justified as simply a natural assumption of any democratic society. Some people view democracy as equivalent to representative democracy. They assume that democracy exists when the public plays its part through voting in periodic elections. Another view of democracy suggests that it is about individuals in communities exercising control on the basis of discussion and rational argument, on the basis of the community arriving at a consensus, and on the basis of as much individual consent as possible. Based on this view, the acid test of democracy in relation to the public sector is the degree of continuity between the needs and aspirations of the public and the activities of the public sector. Therefore, any developments that bring about a closer continuity can be seen as democratising the nature of the public sector. There may be a variety of mechanisms for achieving more continuity, and representative democracy is an important one among them.

Consulting the public and involving them in decision making about the allocation of budgets and the design and delivery of services are important in the broader perspective of democracy. This view is gathering support as a perspective on democracy and the public sector. Although many would say this is how it ought to work, there are serious questions about the feasibility of public involvement and its significance for the deepening of democracy in democratic societies.

ACQUIRING INFORMATION

Consultation and involvement of the public may be used by public sector organisations to open up channels of communication with the public. The managers may open themselves up through these channels to the views and opinions of members of the public. They may use the communication with the public to gain a clearer and more accurate view of what needs and aspirations the public has.

The nature of these communications depends in part on whether involvement is aimed at citizens, current service users, or communities. These are not totally interchangeable ways of describing the public. The scope of communications is likely to be very different in each case. Citizens may be asked for their opinions about how public money should be spent. Service users may be asked about particular services and their needs in relation to them. Leaders of community groups may be asked about community problems. All these groups have important information and views, but they are not precisely the same.

Consulting the public is becoming part of a twin-track approach to defining the issues being addressed by the public sector. First, there is the traditional way through the elected politicians and legislation. The elected politicians may call for action by public sector organisations on particular issues (the environment, community safety, economic regeneration, etc.) and may provide strong support for such action. Second, the public sector organisation may survey citizens to find out just how much concern there is among the general public on these matters and the public's own views. For example, consulting the public about community safety may show that the issue for them is the fear of crime. Consequently, action by public sector organisations is framed by the elected politicians (and the laws they pass) and then focused and targeted by consulting and involving the public.

Another example is consultation of service users. The public sector organisation operates within mandates set by the politicians' laws and policy decisions. At one time this was considered enough for public sector organisations. Now top managers want feedback from service users as well. They want regular information that tells them what service users think and how satisfied they are with the services they are receiving. This is the twin-track approach in service delivery.

Proposals for consultation and involvement of the public often draw objections from inside public sector organisations. It may be pointed out that the public's view may contradict the politicians. Or it may be said that there are conflicts of opinion among members of the public, and that those consulted might not be very representative of others. It is difficult to be sure whether these objections are motivated by a preference for older paternalistic styles of public sector activity, or whether they are concerns motivated by a desire to arrive at the truth of public need.

Experienced top managers do not necessarily accept that attempts at involving the public are going to become bogged down in conflicts. Consultation and involvement may find a consensus. Even if they reveal differences between the public's and politicians' aspirations and opinions, then it is best that they are brought to light. It may be that the politicians have got it wrong, or that the politicians are taking a balanced view and a section of the public are concentrating on their own immediate interests. The elected politicians have the responsibility, in the end, to make judgements about competing priorities and conflicts of interest. That is the purpose of democracy—to resolve the plurality of needs and aspirations. So, in summary, top managers, who support public involvement, argue that the public sector needs to have the public's direct input. They argue that they are better placed to improve the public sector and provide strategic leadership if they know about differences and disagreements. To be ignorant of them might seem easier but would result in a less satisfactory outcome in the end.

More public sector managers have begun to do surveys of service users and the public. Some of them have been carrying out surveys for a long time. The data from surveys may be analysed and reported back to management teams for planning performance improvements. They may be reported back to the public. For example, graphs showing public satisfaction ratings with a service may be presented on posters and displayed where service users can see them. In fact, with the growth of all sorts of consultation and involvement the effort by the public sector to report back to the public has also grown. Newsletters to service users and newspapers sent to households have become quite common. Perhaps there is some hidden law of reciprocity at work here. The public sector managers are feeling under more of an obligation to explain policies and service priorities, and to persuade the public of the need for changes made in public services. The growth of consultation activities on one side, and increased explanations and attempts to convince from the public sector on the other, begin to resemble a process of dialogue with the public about policy and strategic changes. This may be prompted by an attempt to lower public expectations, but it can be inspired by a vision of a more democratic and inclusive society. In the case of local government, a process of dialogue may be seen as an element in the building of community involvement in key decisions about budget allocation, community problem solving, and service delivery.

DECISION MAKING

Public sector managers have been designing, and experimenting with, mechanisms for making aspirations for consultation and involvement in decision-making real. They have looked for ways of deepening involvement. Instead of broad-brush surveys of public opinion, some managers have designed practical processes for consulting service users at different points in the cycle of developing and delivering a service. First, the users are consulted on service design before the service even exists. Then they are consulted at the delivery stage to check how satisfactory the actual service is from a user pespective. Finally, they are consulted afterwards at a review stage to see if the service has produced the desired outcomes intended by politicians. In this way, consultation and involvement can have a closer connection to decision making.

There is a wide range of techniques for consulting and involving service users to inform and impact on decision making. Some common techniques include:

- Surveys
- Satisfaction slips
- User forums
- User panels
- Focus groups
- Complaints procedures
- Ideas schemes

Many public sector organisations seemed to have started with surveys. These have been used in a variety of ways. They may be used to check out public perceptions of the functionality of a service. Service providers may have designed and be delivering the service to achieve one set of results, but the public may be looking for a different set of results and consequently perceive little use or value in the service. Such surveys are used for decisions on performance goals. Surveys may be used to check out the pricing of public services. For example, a public sector organisation may want to know whether it should improve a service and whether the public would be prepared to pay the extra cost of the improved service. In this case the survey results may be used to decide whether to improve the service and by how much the charge of the service should be increased. Surveys may be used for evaluating the impact of improvement plans. This involves using the survey to establish the baseline performance and then a follow-up survey to measure the impact of an improvement on satisfaction and quality from the service user perspective.

Some organisations use multiple methods. They may have started with simple surveys asking service users who had visited the organisation's building for a service. The questions asked could be quite basic ones. What services have you just used? How satisfied are you with them? Are there any changes you would like? They may have experimented with more complex surveys looking at service users' values and attitudes on a range of matters. Then they might have tried out panel surveys. A sample of service users may have been recruited to answer questions every six months or even more frequently. This can help with tracking changes over time, but in fact the respondents may be asked quite different questions each time.

Not only may different types of survey be used. Organisations may add the use of techniques based on face-to-face consultation and small group discussions. Focus groups may be used, for example, to obtain more in-depth and complex service user views. User forums and panels may be created that allow the organisation to offer user representatives support and training. It is sometimes argued that users of public services gain confidence and assertiveness in forums and panels. This may also be aided by offering support and training to service users. In consequence service users become able—some service user advocates would describe this as empowered—to voice their criticisms and challenge providers. Managers sometimes describe these panels and forums as very influential in terms of decisions about how to develop a particular service.

This general picture of service user consultation and involvement needs a little qualification. For a start, not all of this activity began in the 1990s. Some organisations have had processes for involving users for 20 or more years. Secondly, there are problems and frustrations in making user involvement work satisfactorily. Some managers, for example, complain that users are intermittent in their interest. There are peaks of user activity in user panels and participation schemes, followed by periods when involvement is moribund. Sometimes managers say that service users are only being interested in participation when there is an issue or when they can see some personal advantage in being involved. For example, it may be difficult to find service users to volunteer for a forum or panel to discuss general issues, but at particular times there are plenty of volunteers because there is a matter of concern to the service users. Parents may be content to take a distant interest in their children's school normally, but want to be involved and have a say when they think their child's education is suffering. At such times the school's parent–teacher association meeting may be very well attended. Service user involvement can be very uncomfortable for service providers on these occasions of heightened involvement.

Managers sometimes sound as if they disapprove of this personal interest motive and the conflict that sometimes accompanies it, as though the user of a public service has a duty to be interested in the service at all times and only in a general way. In contrast, some public sector managers are keen to see the organisation enter a zone of discomfort in relations with service users. They want service users to be critical about the services provided. This is justified as constructive criticism to make services better. They champion complaint procedures and argue the importance of analysing and reporting on complaints to drive improvements in results. Some organisations have also established idea schemes so that service users' suggestions for improvements can be fed into decision-making processes. These can be simple invitations to service users to write ideas on cards and send them to the organisation.

There are also attempts to increase the involvement of citizens in decision making. One vehicle for this has been the citizen's jury. This is a European idea to have a representative panel of a dozen or so citizens who are asked to hear evidence over a number of days on a particular issue. The panel may be asked to look at a community problem (e.g. drugs) or a service delivery problem (e.g. the distribution of library services). They call witnesses and have the chance to ask the views and opinions of experts. After due deliberation the panel gives its verdict. The idea has been taken up in local government. Top managers in local government see this as a way of finding out what the community thinks.

Forums may be set up for particular sections of citizens such as young people, or women or ethnic minorities. The aim may be to get their views on a range of services. This is again a feature of recent local government experiments and is motivated by a fear that these parts of the community are alienated from the political process and poorly served by public services. These forums can be used to inform management decision making as well as local policy making by elected politicians.

CO-MANAGEMENT AND CO-PRODUCTION

Co-management and co-production are ideas discussed in the North European public management literature. For example, Torben Beck Jorgensen (1993b, p. 223) has described a form of governance, which he calls 'the self-governing state, in which citizens take part in the production process itself, not only as co-producers but also as citizens deciding what is to be produced and under what circumstances'.

There are examples in England of citizens managing public services. Tenant management co-ops have entered into agreements with public sector landlords to carry out the management of their housing. There is evidence from the London borough of Islington in the 1980s that these tenant management co-ops were effective in managing repairs, voids, relet times and rent arrears (Gyford 1991, p. 64). An even larger-scale experiment in citizen involvement in co-management was brought about as a result of educational reforms in the 1980s. In 1988 nearly 100 000 parent governors were elected (Gyford 1991, p. 68). Experiments in co-management continue. A south Somerset town has a swimming pool that was part funded by local government but is run by service users in the town on the basis of charges to those using the swimming pool. The service users are also responsible for the training and provision of lifeguards in the swimming pool. A recent interesting example is that of a self-funding project undertaken by Ashford Borough Council in Kent and completed in 1998. The council got a developer to build and provide the capital for a recreation centre as a planning obligation. The local community was consulted and individuals from the community now form a majority of the group of management trustees. Its activities generate a surplus and the management trust receives a management fee. The community was involved in designing the recreation centre, is represented on the centre's management trust, and has (via the management trust) a say in the development of its activities.

Berman (1998) provides an example of an initiative that goes beyond simply involving citizens or users in managing services. Orange County, Florida, carried out community-based strategic planning in 1995. 'This planning effort aimed to get citizens more involved in their community and to ensure that agencies put the needs and values of citizens first. Agencies examined opportunities to empower citizens to take greater responsibility for their communities as well as to provide better services to citizens and clients' (Berman 1998, p. 167).

MAKING INVOLVEMENT EFFECTIVE

The idea of consulting and involving the public is one that has widespread appeal. The techniques by which service users and citizens may be consulted and involved are widely known. However, there is little basis for complacency about the effectiveness of public consultation and involvement. One UK study of district general managers in the health service found some criticism of an official report that had recommended involving consumers. The managers are reported to have felt that the report 'oversimplified the difficulties of involving consumers, particularly at a time of financial constraint and in the absence of reliable information' (Pettigrew et al. 1992, p. 57). Apparently none of the managers said that involving consumers was an area of achievement.

Effectiveness depends on more than an aspiration to consult and involve the public. It depends on more than knowledge of techniques. It depends on using the right strategies. While there are issues about the conditions within which consultation and involvement take place, this chapter concludes with an examination of organisational strategies for making consultation and involvement effective and an examination of implementation factors.

ORGANISATIONAL STRATEGIES

One corporate approach to improving the effectiveness of consulting and involving the public is to set corporate quality standards. Very large organisations may be able to afford consultation specialists or units to set and monitor corporate standards, as well as provide advice and support on the techniques and methods of consulting and involving the public. Service units are required to submit their proposals for vetting by the corporate specialists or units. The presumption is that meeting these requirements ensures that consultation and involvement are done properly.

Another approach is to persuade service units to adopt self-assessment using the EFQM model for business excellence. The EFQM model can be very appealing to managers and employees for its 'scientific' nature and for its support of diagnostic and problem-solving processes within organisations. One of the elements within that model of quality management is customer satisfaction. If the corporate centre of a public sector organisation can sell the whole idea of the EFQM model then this legitimises paying attention to the public. The EFQM model functions rather like a Trojan horse, helping to introduce a concern for public perceptions across all parts of the organisation.

IMPLEMENTATION FACTORS

If corporate strategies such as those considered above have been applied and there are still poor results from public consultation and involvement then organisations may need to look at implementation factors. Two of the most commonly considered implementation factors are organisational arrangements and the organisation's culture.

The easiest and most obvious way to change an organisational structure to help make consultation and involvement more effective is to employ specialists in working with the public. For example, community development officers may be employed in local government to find out what community needs there are and mobilise community resources or realign public sector activities to meet these needs. Public housing services may employ staff to work with tenants' representatives and give them support and training.

Culture changes are difficult but may also be important for implementation of a policy of consulting and involving the public. The key cultural change is to get the organisation to value the public's aspirations and priorities over those of professionals. But even prior to this cultural change is creating a culture that is aware of service users. It may be felt by top managers that they need to get their organisation to be aware of the public's perspective before they can move on to convincing the organisation that the public needs to be involved in decision making.

The chief barrier to this cultural change is often seen in the public sector as the continued hold of older styles of professional cultures.

In some areas of the public sector it may be assumed that professionals should determine the activities of the organisation and the objectives of the activities. It may be assumed that even feedback by the public is largely unnecessary because the public lacks the specialist knowledge of the professional.

Another important cultural change is that of learning to cope with the discomfort and challenge of a public sector that consults and involves the public. This is a culture that seeks creativity and innovation from willingness to engage in dialogue with the public. It is not a comfortable public sector.

In practice, culture change is often addressed through training programmes for employees. Berman (1998) has described how Orange County, Florida, planned to provide training in customer service to its employees in 1997. Apparently this training was intended to help employees create 'service partnerships' with citizens and clients. It was also designed to deal with the difficult aspects of interacting with the public, such as conflict resolution and resolving service problems.

SUMMARY AND CONCLUSIONS

The public sector is beginning to engage the public in many different ways. This engagement is particularly important around strategic changes. The public needs to be consulted and involved before, during, and after strategic changes. And yet there have been decades of experience in which the public sector has been isolated from the public and none of these things have happened.

In this chapter the reasons for engaging the public have been examined. The public should be consulted and involved in order that the politicians' support can be maintained, the experiences of the public and providers of public services can be understood and related, the services and activities of the public sector can be improved, and the principles of democracy observed. The meaning of consultation and involvement was probed in terms of information, decision making, co-management, and co-production. Finally, the challenge of public consultation and involvement was discussed in terms of organisational strategies, and organisational and cultural changes.

The underlying theme of this chapter has been the tension between the widespread belief, in principle, of consulting and involving the public and the difficulty of doing these things in practice. This may reflect the fact that the public sector is at a turning point—moving from a social democratic paternalism to a new responsiveness based on a populist culture.

12

Partnership Working

INTRODUCTION

Public sector organisations are expected to make use of partnerships to increase their economy, efficiency, and effectiveness. Governments now encourage partnership working to deal with complex problems as well as to enhance service delivery. Partnerships may be formed as loose coalitions of organisations with a commitment to work on defining community problems and identifying shared goals. They may be formally structured with signed agreements on how partners will work together. They may have a legal element. For example, some partnerships are formed by public sector organisations and their suppliers and are designed to enhance the contractual basis of the relationships. Partnerships may be joint ventures between public and private sectors to deliver services. Partnerships have been set up to implement welfare to work schemes, improve social housing, and to obtain and use public money for economic regeneration of localities. They have been used to make regulatory services more effective, to improve co-ordination of health and social services, and to bring together the services of several local authorities in the interests of economy. They have been formed to address the fear of crime in communities, to bring together complementary resources of the public and voluntary sectors in new children's and family services, and to build hospitals. Examples of partnerships can be given from across the whole spectrum of public sector activities.

For chief executives partnership working has meant a significant amount of their working time devoted to meetings with partners. As

Berman (1998, p.135) points out, 'partnerships are often very effective, but they also require considerable management'. It has meant formulating and sanctioning agreements on partnership schemes. It has meant learning to work with a much wider range of organisations than in the past. It has meant working in consortiums that sometimes include organisations with a disparate set of mandates and objectives. For the public sector organisation involved in a number of partnership schemes it has meant learning how to play different roles in different partnerships—the lead partner in one case, a core partner in another, and just a secondary partner in yet another case. As the lead partner in one partnership a public sector organisation may have done all the financial planning, the public relations work, and so on, and other partners may have just put their names to it. In other cases the same organisation may be keen for other organisations to do all the work.

In the late 1990s partnerships became an expression of 'conspicuous production' in some management circles. Some chief executives felt that their credibility depended on having a number of partnership schemes that were well known. Along with conspicuous production went a tendency to say that partnership schemes were working well and were successful. Privately, chief executives would admit that partnership working was difficult in practice. Even where the partners had complementary legal mandates and a commitment to public service, partnerships were difficult.

In the next section of this chapter the purposes of partnership working are outlined. These are the motives or drivers that can cause public sector organisations to attempt partnership working despite the obstacles and barriers to effective partnership working. This is followed by an examination of the activities that go under the banner of partnership working. Finally, the chapter sets out a number of important elements for developing effective partnership working.

THE PURPOSES OF PARTNERSHIP

One big inducement to partnership working is the need to sort out overlapping mandates. Wilkinson & Monkhouse (1994) suggest that this is an important part of the strategic planning process of any organisation. They advise public sector managers to search for the opportunities and threats implied in meeting the demands on their organisations.

> Having identified the various demands that are made of the organization it may be of benefit to take each demand area and to identify other organizations that also service that demand and categorize them according to whether they provide a complementary service to that provided by one's own organization or actually compete in the same service provision. Examples of these categories would be police and ambulance complementing each other in dealing with serious road accidents while police and health service compete in dealing with drug and drink abuse (p. 18).

In the interests of cutting out waste, elected politicians often want to see co-ordination rather than competition between public sector organisations. Of course, top managers of a public sector organisation may be motivated by survival instincts or by empire building and may choose to compete for public resource allocations rather than to work with other public sector organisations to define clear boundaries or to work co-operatively in alliances (Heymann 1987). The case of Denmark's civil defence service in the 1970s is a good illustration of strategies prompted by a desire to survive. The service was threatened by, and experienced, cutbacks. The management response was to adopt 'strategies to avoid further retrenchment. They expanded their activities in cases of fire, environmental pollution, snow storms, storm surges and the like . . . they, by creating a new policy space, faced new competitors guarding their organizational domains: the fire service and the environmental agencies' (Jorgensen 1993a, p. 151).

Sorting out overlapping mandates is considered critical for the improvement of the performance of the public sector. The health and social services in the 1980s and 1990s provided a major example in England. They had overlapping mandates. They shared clients and were in some cases alternative suppliers of public services. For example, the two services shared the same service users, when patients were discharged from hospital after medical treatment and then required support from social services. They were alternative suppliers of long-term care for some client groups.

The respective activities of the health and social services were sometimes difficult to co-ordinate on the basis of defining a clear boundary between them. It is more difficult to distinguish between a health need and a social need than might at first appear. Take the case of someone who is learning disabled living in a home provided by the voluntary sector and funded by social services. If that person is labelled as having challenging behaviour, is this really a problem of poorly trained social care workers who lack appropriate skills to do their job properly or does the person have a mental health problem that requires intervention by psychologists or psychiatrists employed by the health service? In consequence should social services pay for the intervention of the health professionals or is this an expense that the health services should bear? Or, another example might be, if elderly people are in a residential home do they require social care or medical help when they are dementing? A third example could be the choice faced by the parents of a delinquent adolescent who has used physical violence against them—should they call on the services of social workers or health service psychiatrists (or the police)?

These ambiguities have at times necessitated negotiations by managers over both the provision of services and the responsibility for paying for them. So public sector managers have spent time negotiating which organisation would do what for service users and how the service would be paid for. The drafting of eligibility criteria and admissions protocols sought to rationalise who received what care from whom. For instance, in the social services and health services case there were continuing care criteria to decide who was responsible for funding a service. But such criteria still have to be interpreted and applied and did not result in a clear separation of responsibilities and activities of health and social services personnel. Naturally, then, there were suggestions that health and social services personnel should work together in the interests of the public.

Partnership working by public agencies may be encouraged by national governments to avoid duplication and waste. This can be seen particularly in the case of tiers of government. Partnerships between the tiers may be set up to eliminate the duplication of activities. Economies in sharing activities may also be sought. For example, shared access points for the public not only make life easier for the public seeking information or wanting a service, but also cut down on the expenses for the partner organisations.

Partnerships can also be a response to a competitive situation. Large parts of the public sector became more exposed to competitive pressures in the 1980s and early 1990s. One way of dealing with competition is to differentiate the activities of an organisation from others like it. Many universities, for example, now see themselves in sharp competition for students. This includes foreign students. It has been pointed out that the global market in students is a significant one and marketing of courses overseas has been expanded substantially in recent years. This intense rivalry in the market for students may be managed to some degree by partnership working between universities to develop complementary strengths.

The boundary between sectors is now blurring. The difference between education and employment is one example of this. Traditional universities are becoming more conscious of the rivalry of corporate universities. Major global companies are creating universities to develop the skills of their employees. If companies provide their own educational services must this mean a diminished market for traditional universities? The corporate universities are seen as a threat. Some universities might see partnerships with companies to provide off-campus degrees as a way of heading off this threat by obviating the need for educational provision by companies and by learning as quickly as possible what it is the companies feel they may have to provide themselves.

Partnerships may be motivated by a desire to access funding and other resources. Substantial sums of public money have been made available on a competitive bidding basis and consortiums have been formed to make bids. For example, regeneration funding on this basis has led to partnerships between the public, private, and voluntary sectors. Capital projects have also been carried out as public–private partnerships to take advantage of government initiatives in England. The provision of public money for partnership working has been a big incentive for public sector organisations to seek out private sector partners. Public sector managers have complained repeatedly about budget cutbacks and a lack of money for new initiatives. The desire to access additional funding has led them to explore innovative ideas to access government funding, and to develop expertise in putting together packages of proposals based on partnerships, funding requirements, and the needs of the public. The provision of public money has been an incentive for private sector companies to consider the potential of profitable partnership activity with the public sector.

An individual organisation may also seek to improve its results by gaining access to skills lodged in other organisations and using them to address needs important to the organisation's goals.

In the face of financial constraints organisations have also looked for partnerships to share the cost of an initiative or service. Some local councils, for instance, which have economic regeneration goals, have created partnerships with the private sector and jointly funded the promotion and marketing of town centres and tourism.

Partnerships may be seen as a way of catalysing community action and this may be seen as offering savings for the public purse. Social services may form partnerships with the voluntary sector in order to promote more community-based support networks, thereby reducing the demands on statutory services. The more the community does to support independent living by elderly people, for example, the longer it is before they need residential services.

Some chief executives argue that partnerships are now essential. They say they cannot conceive of operating without partnerships. This may reflect the interdependence of their organisations with other public sector organisations. A hospital providing medical services in the centre of London has to plan and manage the use of its hospital beds very carefully. It needs to have a good knowledge of how many people are using the beds, their length of stay in hospital, and the balance between patients needing beds for a short period and those needing beds for longer periods. They need this information to manage the flow of people into the hospital and the flow of them going home. This management process is not only complex, it is also critical for operational effectiveness. If the relatively small numbers occupying beds for a long time increases significantly, the numbers of patients that can be admitted to the hospital falls drastically. The partnership with agencies providing support to someone who has just returned from a period in hospital has obvious and deep implications for the operational effectiveness of the hospital. Partnership working by managers in the hospital and by managers in local government is, consequently, important.

Partnerships have also become important as a result of the emergence of cross-cutting issues that do not fall naturally into alignment with public sector structures inherited from times past. Perhaps restructuring in the longer term will obviate the need for partnerships within the public sector, but there are managers who see partnerships with the private and voluntary sectors as continuing to be essential by virtue of the nature of these new social issues. Therefore, they say that partnership working is now necessary if the public sector is to serve the public and promote the well-being of the community. This is a strong motive—this public service ethos. There is a powerful commitment to promoting the interests of the public. Top managers are therefore willing to experiment and learn how to play their part in these new partnership processes. This can mean for public sector chief executives quite new activities of sharing leadership, sharing ideas, being creative, and agreeing agendas or objectives to shape not just the short term but also medium- and long-term joint activities.

PARTNERSHIP PROCESSES

Partnership working is about co-operating with other organisations. This co-operation can take the form of two or more public service organisations presenting a joint face and joint approach to working for the public. They have to find mechanisms for linking together what they communicate to the public and for linking together their activities.

A different form of partnership process is presented by a public sector organisation working on issues with other organisations that are stakeholders. In this case, partnership processes are a mechanism for problem solving. This calls for forums in which public managers create a dialogue with stakeholders, negotiate priorities and values, and develop relationships. The issues may be generated by the impact of the organisation's activities, or the pressures the organisation is under in trying to meet its strategic goals. Organisations may suffer from pressures due to an excess of demand for service that cannot be supplied or to budgetary gaps. But they can also be community issues. Top managers may be found fostering partnerships on issues of economic development and regeneration, unemployment, improvements in environmental standards, equality of opportunity, crime and disorder, and quality of life generally. For the public sector organisation the overriding values to be pursued through problem solving come down to creating benefits for the public.

The impetus to deal with an issue may originate with a political objective. Politicians may respond to the recognition of an issue (e.g. unemployment) by formulating a policy. The implementation of this policy in public sector organisations may lead to new services. But it may also require the setting up of partnership schemes.

The process of setting up a partnership is quite different from an organisation developing a new service. The top managers have to do quite different things. Leaders of other organisations have to be approached and convinced of the advantages of working together.

Some of the persuading and convincing of partners must be about the benefits of making a contribution to partnership working. But there may also be a social responsibility argument. Public sector managers may say to private sector leaders that they have a responsibility to contribute skills and resources to tackling community issues. They may target their efforts at persuading and convincing partners by concentrating on influential leaders among private and voluntary sector stakeholders. For the task of public sector managers may be easier to accomplish if they can create champions of partnership working in the other sectors.

In selecting the right partners the public sector managers have to think about the assets and capabilities of the potential partner organisations and how they could be assembled and deployed in a partnership activity. During the process of working together the public sector managers have to work out mechanisms for monitoring progress and providing help to partners when difficulties are encountered. The spirit of partnership working is, after all, a co-operative win–win one, even if some of the partners have fairly conventional commercial objectives. And as the partnership evolves they may have to approach other organisations and enlist their co-operation.

Partnership working is not just an inter-organisational phenomenon. Public sector managers who have pioneered partnership working have found that there is a big job to be done on the internal marketing of partnership working. This may be particularly the case in relation to professionals who are steeped in existing ways of carrying out activities. For example, some regulatory activities by government may make use of partnership working to achieve higher levels of compliance though education and support, whereas some professional sentiments may suggest that the balance of work must continue to stress inspection and prosecution.

Because partnership working is comparatively new in many parts of the public sector it is often experienced as difficult. Its novelty puts a premium on the capacity of managers to contemplate and handle innovation. Bidding for public money for regeneration funding, for example, challenged the existing skills of organisations that were versed in service delivery and traditional public accountability mechanisms. They had to develop very rapidly skills in project design and management and in partnership working. On top of this it required some imaginative thinking about feasible actions to tackle regeneration.

Partnership working has also required the development of new conflict management and risk management processes. Partnerships between different parts of the public sector have often been far from plain sailing. Various differences in the operating environments of the different agencies or services create difficulties. For example, there are differences in budgetary allocation processes and financial pressures, differences in professional culture, differences in the objectives of managers and reporting arrangements, and differences in executive decision-making and planning processes. The conflict-handling processes are needed to cope with the recurrent blockages to effective partnership from whichever side of the partnership relationship they originated. Some of these conflicts arise when there are overlapping mandates and arguments about the effects of a partner organisation's decisions. A decision to cut back a service because of a gap in next year's budget may mean less support for another public agency that has been using the service in question. A decision by a hospital to reduce the time for patients to remain in hospital after an operation so that it can increase its efficiency shifts cost to its local social services department that may have to face increasing demand for support by people returning home.

Risk management processes were needed for public–private partnerships in which funding was being managed through long-term contracts. For example, the public sector partner has to make careful calculations of value for money and risk over the life of the contract. This makes new demands on the skill and expertise of public sector management. The use of techniques of sensitivity analysis and the modelling of the effects of decisions are used to ensure that the public stands a good chance of benefiting from contracts with the private sector where the latter is primarily motivated by an attractive commercial return.

EFFECTIVE PARTNERSHIPS

There are a number of ingredients that go into successful partnership working. These comprise:

- Creating a partnership agenda
- Selecting an organisational form
- Forming a partnership plan
- Focusing partnerships on achievement
- Developing appropriate skills

Creating a partnership agenda

Different types of public sector organisation have different possibilities for creating a partnership agenda. One of the most frequently discussed in recent years has been the use by local authorities of community planning. 'Partnerships often follow in the wake of community-based strategic planning process' (Berman 1998, p. 134). Indeed, the strategic planning on a community basis creates strategic alliances as local organisations come together to identify and then solve community problems. The alliances are needed to implement the community plans.

Chief executives in many local authorities have done work on community plans. These may be defined as built around a set of agreed priorities for a community. These priorities may emerge in part on the basis of large-scale surveys of members of the public. But local authorities may also create partnership forums or consortiums consisting of local private and voluntary sector organisations to work out community priorities.

The actual mechanics of developing an agenda are not complicated. The local authority can organise workshops or events with the support of process facilitators to work out the strategic issues facing a local community. The development of a community plan obviously requires more than that a set of issues be identified. For example, partners may want to agree on how addressing these issues will contribute to a shared vision of a successful and prosperous community. They will certainly need to think about how the issues might be tackled and which partners will work on which issues.

The workshops or events may be supported by research. For example, if crime and safety are issues for a local community, then the local authority may find it helpful to collect statistics on crime in the area and survey public opinion. The results of such research can be reported as part of a workshop or event. The statistical data and public opinion, together with expert advice from the local police service, can be used to define the problem that needs addressing. The partners can work towards a statement of the problem, before beginning to work out how the activities of all the partners can be realigned so as to tackle the problem. At the same time, the partners can set up liaison and monitoring mechanisms to ensure the strategy of the partners is being implemented.

Public sector organisations that are leading, or partners in, community planning should consider the links between the community plan and their own strategic plan. The result will be a degree of co-alignment between the strategic plans of the public sector organisations co-operating in community planning. Internally, the public sector organisation can end up with four different types of planning all co-aligned: community planning, strategic planning, performance planning (setting annual performance targets based on performance indicators), and improvement planning (identifying improvement goals in response to reported performance gaps). Figure 12.1 depicts the alignment of different planning processes with community planning forming the foundation.

A very different approach is to create a partnership agenda by using community development workers. The emphasis in this case is not on strategy processes but on community involvement. Public sector organisations begin by setting up a project and then recruiting community development professionals to work on it. Their initial work is to 'scout' the community and map the organisations and groupings that exist. They then proceed by building strong links with the organisations and groupings that seem to be relevant to the project.

The aim in this case is not so much to solve a problem in the community as to develop the community. The emphasis is on getting organisations and groups involved in practical measures of benefit to them. There may be some small sums of money to support and help organisations and groups do what they want to do.

Building partnerships for community action of this nature seems to be intrinsically difficult to steer strategically by top management of a public organisation. The community development workers operate quite autonomously. Ensuring the output from partnership working feeds into some overarching set of strategic priorities is problematic when it is based on professional community development activity. It also seems likely that it will be less effectively

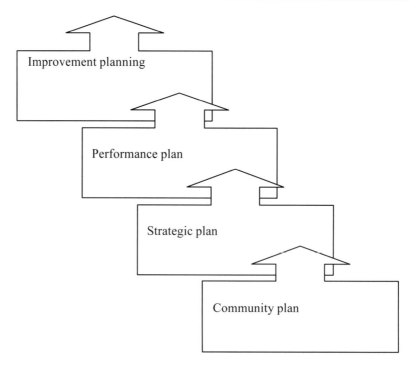

Figure 12.1 Community plan and other plans

monitored simply because community development as an end in itself is the goal rather than action to solve community problems.

Selecting an organisational form

Various organisational forms are possible for partnership working. The partnership may be merely an informal agreement to co-operate or co-ordinate efforts. The partnership may be formed between an organisation and one of its suppliers with the aim of using the partnership working to enhance the effectiveness of the commercial contract. However, partnerships may also be project based or expressed in a joint venture structure.

A project form of organisation is common where financing has been obtained as result of a bid for discretionary government funding. Projects are appropriate for innovative activities that have been funded for a specific period of time.

Joint ventures may be used for service-related activities. These can be useful for situations in which the public sector organisation recognises that there are skills or capabilities held by a private sector organisation that it does not have and it is interested in acquiring these over a period of time. It may also be used for partnerships between public sector organisations where they have decided to pool their resources and gain economies of scale.

Forming a partnership plan

For more formal partnership organisations there is a lot to be sorted out. What assets are the various partners contributing? What services and facilities can the partnership access from the partners? What benefits will partners gain? Who will control and manage partnership activities? How will decisions be made? How will disagreements be handled? How will the performance of the partnership be reviewed? How long will the partnership continue? A plan covering all these questions needs to be drawn up and agreed.

Focusing partnerships on achievement

Partnerships may not achieve what they are intended to achieve. They may be a disappointment. This can occur for a variety of reasons. First, there may be a phoney convergence of agendas or interests among the partners based on rhetoric of shared aims and public service. In practice, the partners may continue to pursue their own unrelated interests while paying lip-service to partnership working. Second, there may have been inaccurate perceptions of the abilities or assets being brought to the partnership by one or more of the partners. In consequence, the results are just not very good. Third, some partners may be just dipping a toe in partnership working. They may not be convinced of the payoffs of partnership working but are curious enough to go along with the idea for a while. Because they are not really serious, however, they may make little contribution and do not make much effort to make it a success. These various reasons may, of course, cause the partnership working to disintegrate after a while as it becomes obvious that little is being achieved.

Therefore, public sector managers need to be alert to 'in principle' support from partners in meetings. They need to be alert to people taking part in partnership meetings for the sake of being involved. Partnerships need to be focused on achievement. Otherwise, partnership schemes degenerate into a ritual with no real function from the point of view of public service.

Developing appropriate skills

The public sector managers responsible for developing and sustaining partnership working need a wide range of skills if this is to be effective.

There are various skills needed for handling social relationships. These include leadership skills. In some cases the public sector organisation needs to be leading the partnership processes. This may be very challenging when the partners are other parts of the public sector and there is a history of organisational rivalry. It may also be very challenging when the partners are private business leaders and there has been limited contact in the past, so that there is not a pre-existing basis of trust and understanding. The public sector obviously has a special part to play in leading partnership working because of its mandate to serve the public and because of the democratic legitimacy of the role of elected politicians within the public sector.

Alongside skills in leading, public sector managers need skills in performing an enabling role through partnership working. This involves exploring with partners the resources and needs that could be matched up to produce better results. In partnership working this matching-up process is done voluntarily and co-operatively. The public sector cannot direct or order partners to do it. These skills are increasingly important as the public sector recognises that not all problems can be addressed through direct public sector provision. The public sector managers, therefore, work increasingly by enabling the community to exploit better its own resources.

Joint decision-making skills are evidently important in partnership processes. This applies to the public sector chief executive. He or she is often operating alongside other chief executives in steering groups and consortium bodies and then liaising over the implementation of the decisions and agreements reached within them. The chief executive is not just an ambassador making purely diplomatic contact with others. There are also joint decision-making skills being used in strategic planning by partner organisations. At the operational level too there is a need for more joint decision-making skills as a result of cross-boundary management activities. The increasing use of contracts within the public sector and pressures towards 'joined up' government call for more discussions with managers in other organisations. They need to sort problems laterally rather than refer issues upwards.

Skills in making decisions within collective problem-solving arenas are also important. Large-scale events involving 50 or even several hundred people may call for chief executives and top management teams to respond to discussion and feedback and then make decisions in public. This is a form of joint decision making with its very own unique dynamics. It is about as far removed as you can imagine from the situation of a chief executive sitting behind his or her desk making decisions.

Partnership working requires conflict-handling skills to deal with, for instance, rivalry among partners. Different parts of the public sector may be required to work together to serve the public but there are plenty of differences that can become the basis of rivalry and 'turf wars'. This may not take place on an enormous scale, but it is often present and needs managing.

SUMMARY AND CONCLUSIONS

More and more public sector organisations are expected to work with other organisations. Partnerships are being formed with other public sector organisations, as well as with organisations in the private and voluntary sectors.

There seem to be many good arguments for partnership working. The most powerful is that partnership working can improve the results achieved by the public sector. This is partly a matter of overcoming the problems of overlapping mandates and blurred boundaries. It is also about coping with financial constraints and seeking to access more resources. In some cases partnership working is seen as essential if there is to be any prospect of tackling serious community issues. Some top public sector managers see it as a natural way of promoting the well-being of the community.

The processes of partnership working have been examined. Partnerships as a way of co-operating with other organisations and as an approach for problem solving were considered. Other processes also explored were: setting up a partnership, working together with partners, internal marketing, project design and management, conflict management, and risk management.

Finally, some consideration was given to what activities are needed for successful partnership working. Five were selected for discussion: creating a partnership agenda, selecting an organisational form, forming a partnership plan, focusing partnerships on achievement, and developing appropriate skills.

13
Opening Up

Some public sector managers do see what they are attempting to do on the external communications front as more than simply listening and finding out what the public wants. They use phrases such as 'opening up' their organisation and 'connecting' with the public. They may stress the need for 'open-mindedness' when asking the public for opinions and views and listening to ideas. This can be contrasted with the paternalistic state where the politicians and professionals believed they knew what was best for the public. The politicians had their political doctrines and professionals had their professional expertise. Perhaps this explains why public sector organisations were bureaucratic. Because the politicians and professionals believed that they knew best there was no need to communicate with the public or enter into a dialogue about what the public needed or wanted. So the isolation of the bureaucratic organisation probably reinforced or was caused by the paternalism.

Opening up is defined here as the process of developing an organisation that is accountable, responsive, and a learning organisation. In this chapter we look at both the democratic argument and the performance argument for opening up public sector organisations. Together they provide a pragmatic philosophy of the process of the transition of public sector organisations under modernisation.

Three different processes of opening up are examined in turn. First, accountability processes are looked at in terms of performance measurement arrangements and honesty. Then processes of responding to the public, service users, and partners are outlined. Finally, the processes used by a learning organisation are considered. These are learning by making external comparisons and optimising readiness to learn.

Some methods of increasing the effectiveness of opening up public sector organisations are reviewed. These are classified as training, unlearning old ideas, developing managers, building the confidence of managers, and encouraging entrepreneurial activity.

ARGUMENTS FOR OPENING UP

A common theme of criticisms of public sector organisations is that they are too bureaucratic. This means in part that they are isolated from the public that they are meant to serve. This is reflected in concerns that they have been to a large degree unaccountable to the public apart from the indirect accountability based on the periodic election of politicians. So opening up a public sector organisation means opening it up to be influenced by the public. By extension it also means opening it up to the influence of private and voluntary sector organisations formed by members of the public.

There is often an assumption that democracy should be increased to counter bureaucracy. This can mean improving the democracy of voting. But there is a wider idea of democracy. In Chapter 11 it was suggested that the democratic character of the public sector could be measured by the degree of continuity between the needs and aspirations of the public and the activities of the public sector. Actions and processes that produce more continuity can therefore be regarded as democratising the public sector. Consequently, initiatives to open up public sector organisations to the influence of the public's views of its needs and aspirations are part of a democratisation agenda.

A shift towards listening to the public is an important aspect of this opening up. A process of opening up can aid the realisation of a better public sector because it allows organisations to gain access to ideas. This is obviously one of the benefits of listening to the public. This may be done by a public sector organisation seeking to work with its stakeholders on tackling issues. There are efforts to widen the range of views and perspectives heard and to encourage people to give their ideas on how issues could be addressed. There is a presumption in this that effective problem-solving behaviour requires more creativity and an acceptance that managers and professionals in the public sector do not have all the answers.

More democracy could also be produced by an entrepreneurial public sector. Having listened to the public and taken note of its needs and aspirations, there is a requirement for a response. Listening alone is not enough. In the context of bureaucratic conditions, there is a premium on entrepreneurial management, which has ambitions for meeting the needs of the public and a capability that mobilises resources and constructs alliances (Osborne & Gaebler 1992).

Within existing public sector organisations there are moves already to more entrepreneurial management. At times this appears to be a style of management aimed mainly at making a difference in a bureaucratic situation. Being entrepreneurial is seen as flexibility rather than creativity, and quickness rather than innovation. Entrepreneurial managers may be seen as having a can-do mentality rather than an inspiring ambition to serve the public better. They work on a shoestring and cobble together alliances to get things done rather than forming strategic alliances to transform performance.

ACCOUNTABILITY PROCESSES

Elected politicians have wanted to make the public sector more accountable. This may be seen as requiring a process for making the top managers accountable to politicians. Early experiments in New Zealand, for example, made the chief executives of government departments more accountable to their ministers. In that case and in the United States, accountability to politicians has been based on performance management ideas. Making managers of government departments and federal agencies accountable was seen to require explicit performance goals and measurement. Then the public sector can be held to account for performance gaps that are knowable and transparent. Certainly in the case of the United States the emphasis on accountability of federal agencies turned the spotlight on data capacity and the reporting of performance to politicians.

To some extent the mere fact of publishing performance plans and having to give reports to politicians has increased the transparency of the public sector for the public. At the very least, the process and results of accountability can be reported in the media. Performance plans of federal agencies may be (and have been) put on the World Wide Web, thereby putting important information about missions and goals in the public domain.

In England there has been a trend towards politicians requiring public services to report and publish performance data. The performance of large parts of the public sector important to the public is now more transparent to the public. Health service data on performance is published. Schools have to publish the examination results of their pupils which allows parents to make more informed judgements about the performance of schools and to which school they wish to send their children. Local authorities have been reporting performance indicators for a number of years, and from the year 2000 onwards have a statutory duty to publish annually a local performance plan as the main mechanism for reporting performance to the public.

There has been some evolution in what performance data is reported and published. In the late 1980s there was a strong emphasis on waiting times as a measure of performance of the health service. More sensitive performance data has now been published. In 1999 the Health Secretary published performance data for hospitals on the Internet—including the mortality rates after surgery for every hospital. This was extensively covered in the media. It was reported that it was the result of almost two years' work by the health service. Even so, 30 per cent of hospital trusts had reported poor or mediocre data. The leader of Britain's hospital consultants was reported as saying that the published performance data left much to be desired and could put consultants under pressure. He was also quoted as saying, 'We don't want doctors to refuse treatment to patients because they are looking over their shoulders to see where they are coming in the figures' (*Evening Standard*, 16 June 1999). Only months earlier there had been a scandal because of a surgeon's high mortality rates in a Bristol hospital in the south-west of England.

The fact that elected politicians have had their civil servants collect and publish data or require public sector organisations to publish performance data does not mean that there is a sustained and intense debate among all members of the public on public sector performance. Nor does it mean that public sector managers are yet under a great deal of pressure to explain to the public what has been done and what their performance plans are for the future. But the trends towards transparency in recent years has made managers more performance conscious and the dangers of a media scandal or of acquiring a reputation for chronic under-performance have increased. Hiding poor performance is no longer as easy as it once was. Perhaps the politicians see the changes they have made as valuable in increasing the pressures to improve results even if direct accountability to the public remains a weak process.

The discussion of performance indicators and performance league tables seems to imply that accountability to the public depends only on formal mechanisms. Some (but not by any means all) top public sector managers identify the importance of honesty as a dimension of the relationship with the public. They say there is a need for more honesty. The issue is often raised in connection with resource constraints. There is an element of defensiveness in this way of putting the arguments for greater honesty. What they mean is that they have been making cuts in services and feel that they are covering up this fact. They would like to see a public awareness that a cut in budgets must, in their view, mean a cut in the extent or quality of services. It is certainly an uncomfortable situation for a manager to be cutting inputs to a service and pretending that the service has not really changed. It is particularly difficult if there are statutory inspection systems and audits to check on performance and quality. The real problem, however, is that politicians are expecting a level of innovation and a shift from a 'tax and spend' mentality that means there should be no simple correlation between tax spend and benefits for the public. They are expecting managers to introduce innovations that increase productivity and partnership working to eliminate waste and access private and voluntary sector resources.

RESPONDING TO THE PUBLIC, SERVICE USERS AND PARTNERS

Being responsive to the public is as important to the opening up of public sector organisations as is being accountable. The first step in being responsive is listening to the public. In order to listen, public sector managers need to create channels for communication or forums in which the public can express their opinions and ideas. The managers and professionals of the public sector can use these to ask the public and service users what they think and what their needs are.

Providing the listening and open-minded approach to dialogue with the public results in changes and improvements, the opening up of the public sector to the influence of the public will have created responsiveness in the public sector. This could amount to a virtuous circle of listening and responding. This would be a virtuous circle to underpin the drive to continuous improvement so frequently sought nowadays in the public sector.

As the public sector engages with the public, they are trying out more ways of listening and finding out what is needed. Large-scale surveys are an obvious starting point because it is possible to prescribe the use of samples that are statistically 'representative'. But the data and its analysis do not lend themselves well to the aims of listening and responding. The whole thing keeps the public too much at arms' length. As the desire to 'connect' becomes stronger (e.g. connecting with young people) and concerns for community issues (e.g. environmental pollution) become more important to the public sector, then new ways of listening and engaging the public are sought. Forums and focus groups may then be tried to get closer to the public. It becomes more acceptable to enter into dialogue with community groups and interest groups and there is less nervousness about the representativeness of the public views sampled. The public sector organisation becomes more sophisticated in its methodology for taking account of a range of views and perspectives. The reliability and validity of different methods of listening and hearing from the public are understood and weighted in arriving at an analysis of what is needed or what aspirations exist among the public.

Initially on opening up the public sector organisation the existence of a multiplicity of interests (stakeholders) is very challenging. Bureaucratic forms of organisation that are not opened up do not deal with this multiplicity of interests. In the case of the bureaucracy the providers of public services were not in communication with the public, were relatively unaware of the complexity of the public, and could ignore the diversity of viewpoints that exist. Perhaps this explains some of the character of the change from administrative structures of the old bureaucratic public sector to the new management structures of the modern public sector. Administrators implemented policies; they left the politics to the politicians and so could ignore how different parts of the public reacted to the activities of the public sector. When public sector organisations open up to the public then they need management and not just administration in order to deal with complexity and ambiguity created by the multiplicity and diversity of interest. Universities, for example, have many interest or stakeholder groups: there are students, government, employers of students, commercial clients who purchase research, consultancy, and education, suppliers, the local community, and so on. Each of these interest or stakeholder groups will have a different idea of how universities should behave and the strategic goals they should pursue. Top managers in universities now have to engage much more with these stakeholders and form the university mission out of a variety of ideas about what it should be doing.

LEARNING ORGANISATIONS

It was suggested above that opening up involved asking questions and listening to the public in an open-minded way. This open-mindedness obviously related to the definition of the public needs to be met and how these needs might be met through the operations of the public sector organisation. However, the bureaucratic public sector organisation has been closed-minded not only in its relations to the public but also in its ability to learn from its external environment. In some parts of the public sector there has been significant reluctance to learn from the successful experiences of other public sector organisations.

It has been suggested that strategic planning in the public sector should make use of benchmarking to check on performance:

> Comparators may exist as similar organizations (possibly operating in a different region) or as sister organizations within the same public sector. Being born of government and, therefore, publicly accountable, they are more inclined to publish their performance measures than their more secretive cousins of the private persuasion. Relevant comparators must be selected to allow comparative analysis of performance and the setting of the critical benchmarks against which the performance of one's own organisation can be judged (Wilkinson & Monkhouse 1994, p. 19).

There has been a lack of interest in making benchmarking studies. This has now changed in many parts of the public sector. Holloway et al. (1999) report the results of British surveys showing relatively high levels of interest in benchmarking in the public sector. Managers have begun making use of performance and cost data. But in many organisations the managers were dubious about the value of learning from benchmarking studies. Some top managers suggest that there is a degree of defensiveness in this attitude. Managers will argue that their organisation's performance may appear to be worse or their costs higher but suggest that the comparisons are misleading. Special factors may be adduced for why the comparison is not possible. Or the managers will attack the performance data itself. This can be very frustrating for top managers who would like to see middle managers using benchmarking studies to make improvements and increase the rate of innovation. Consequently managers in the public sector have been slow to learn from experiences of other organisations, and slow to develop performance data by which to manage improvements. Indeed, performance data has been mainly developed, in England anyway, for purposes of accountability and not for purposes of learning and managing improvements.

INTER-ORGANISATIONAL RELATIONS

In the process of opening up to the public and a range of stakeholders there are two further dimensions—opening up in order to connect better with other parts of the public sector and opening up to competition.

Co-operating and co-ordinating with other parts of the public sector call for the same qualities of listening, open-mindedness in asking questions, and responsiveness that have been considered above.

Opening up to competition has become an issue for the public sector because the politicians have used competition to crack the isolation of public sector bureaucracies. There is an element of competition with private and voluntary sector organisations that has been created by the elected politicians. But other forms of competition have also been used. Public sector organisations now compete by making bids for extra resources. The competitive element in the public sector can cause managers to be reluctant to co-operate and work in partnership. But opening up to competition is being made a tool of modernisation, and is not currently seen as an end in itself.

HOW IS OPENING UP DONE MORE EFFECTIVELY?

Some methods of increasing the effectiveness of opening up public sector organisations are:

- Training
- Unlearning old ideas
- Developing managers
- Building the confidence of managers
- Encouraging entrepreneurial activity

Training

One way to support the process of opening up is by training managers and employees in empathy and listening. Some professions that work in the public sector, such as social workers, are encouraged by their training to think about how they interact with clients. They learn skills in listening and trying to understand. This has traditionally been an aspect of the service delivery process for social workers. But there are other professionals and other employees who have received very little in the way of training for listening to the public.

Unlearning old ideas

There may also be a need to break down some aspects of professional thinking. Some professionals in the public sector do present a strong image of thinking they know best. The public is quick to pick up signs of paternalistic attitudes and resent the way that old-style professionals think they can tell the public the way it will be. These attitudes can also cause them to be very resistant to changes based on partnership working and being responsive to public aspirations. There is a need for efforts to encourage these employees to unlearn old-style professional values.

Developing managers

Opening up requires a shift from an administration ethos. The introduction of management is critical for this shift. Managers are needed, as noted above, to deal with the complexities of recognising and listening to a range of stakeholder interests.

Building the confidence of managers

If an organisation has acquired managers, and has made progress in displacing the administrative ethos that characterised much of the public sector in the past, there is a need to build their confidence for the challenge of dealing with multiple interests. There is also a need to build up the confidence of managers to deal with the competition aspect of opening up.

Encouraging entrepreneurial activity

Finally, the public sector is encouraging managers to use more entrepreneurial activity as a way of fostering the opening-up process. This includes forming partnerships and getting in touch with the public. This is seen as a departure from traditional styles of working in the public sector and there is still a need to identify the distinctive elements of entrepreneurial activity in the public sector and encourage it (Osborne & Gaebler 1992; Leadbetter & Goss 1998). Entrepreneurial government is a major responsibility of management as part of the modernisation process. Opening up through entrepreneurial activity means opening up the public sector to allow the public more say in what needs are being addressed. It also means opening up public sector organisations to allow use to be made of resources from the private sector, from the voluntary sector, and, indeed, from the whole of civil society and all its members. In other words, entrepreneurial activity in the public sector is focused on bringing together and combining a wider range of resources to meet existing public needs better and to meet new public needs (see Figure 13.1).

SUMMARY AND CONCLUSIONS

Opening up the public sector organisation has been placed in the context of arguments about democracy and the need to achieve

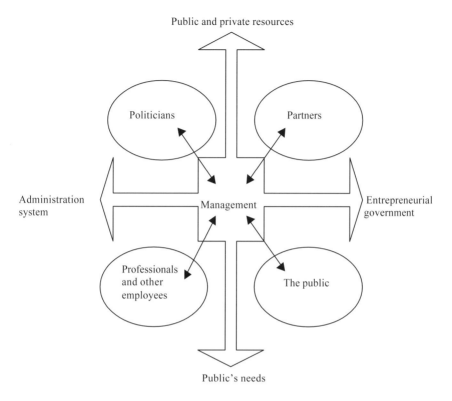

Figure 13.1 Opening up the organisation

better results. Opening up can help with the latter aim by increasing the supply of ideas to the public sector—about the needs and aspirations of the public, for example. It also means constructing alliances and putting resources together in the public interest.

Opening up as a process has been explored in more detail by looking at accountability processes, listening and responding to the public, and the development of an ability and readiness to learn from benchmarking studies.

Actions to increase the effectiveness of the opening-up process include the possibility of using training in empathy and listening, unlearning old-style professional attitudes, developing managers and their confidence, and the encouragement of entrepreneurial activity.

14
In Touch with the Public

INTRODUCTION

The aim of this final chapter is to provide an overall account of strategic change in the public sector. Having explored all the major parts of the strategic change process, it is time to reconsider the strategic change process as a whole once again. The benefit of this is that it allows us to see the function of strategic change for public sector managers in the years ahead. This entails some consideration of the role of strategic management from the point of view of the key problems of the public sector. The implicit theme is that strategic management is a mechanism for integrating change into the operations of the public sector, and, if its promise is fulfilled, this mechanism will spell the end of change through crisis in favour of institutionalised strategic change (Joyce 1998).

This account of strategic change is based on an analysis and interpretation of many developments both inside and outside public sector organisations. It provides a picture of the causes, requirements, and consequences of strategic change in the public sector. As such it offers a map of the context in which individual managers may be seeking to manage the detail of strategic change in the years ahead.

THE CONDITIONS OF STRATEGIC CHANGE

The public sector is a very politicised world. While private sector strategic management can find itself in the middle of political controversy, this happens rarely so easily as in the public sector. The results of public sector activities are often controversial. For example, a reported increase in the proportions of school-leavers achieving good results in public examinations is as likely to result in claims that standards are declining as in congratulations to the schools for their efforts. The public services may themselves be controversial. Is community care about enabling people to live socially valued lives in the community, or the state dumping its responsibilities and putting ordinary members of the public at risk?

Controversy shades into scandals in the public sector. Scandals erupt when social workers fail to intervene and remove children at risk from families, and they are castigated for being too quick to take children away in other cases. Controversy is also linked to improper political motives in the public sector. This may concern the decisions of governments. Changes in UK energy policy in the 1980s, for example, were presented as a matter of economics, but were suspected by many of being a politically motivated act of revenge on the miners' union for events in the 1970s. Controversy over appointing senior civil servants in government departments has its nuance of improper political motives—on both sides of the argument. There are suspicions, on one side, that civil service professionalism hides politically biased attitudes and that civil servants are dragging their feet and impeding the democratic will of the people. The making of political appointments may be justified as the politicians wanting reliable advice, loyalty, and enthusiasm for the politician's objectives. But there are complaints by those who fear that making too many political appointments will destroy the traditional impartiality of public servants.

Despite the politicised nature of the public sector it is sometimes argued that the public is powerless to affect the public sector. This is not true. The public counts in the public sector—but often it counts only in the end. It counts more quickly with elected politicians. Politicians make the public matter to chief executives and other senior executives in public sector organisations.

The public has an impact on politicians even when it is being apathetic. Politicians worry about the health of democracy, fear public apathy, and are concerned about the poor value the public is getting from public sector organisations. Rebuilding public support and revitalising public services are at the top of many politicians' agendas. And the politicians make sure that it is at the top of the agenda of those who lead public sector organisations. Rebuilding public confidence is seen as requiring improved public sector performance, which is seen as necessitating the modernising of public sector management. The politicians are paying attention to surveys that show that trust in public services is slumping. This crisis in public trust and satisfaction appears to be international.

Modernising public sector management, improving performance, and thus changing the public's attitudes towards public sector organisations is not easy. Current efforts to change public sector management and improve performance are not the first. Large-scale efforts in these areas now stretch back 15 or 20 years in many countries. Governments have applied considerable pressure to public services. They have been setting clear performance goals for government departments and introducing performance measurement regimes. They have been looking for efficiency gains. They have challenged the public sector to do more with less. Politicians have said that governments must perform much better than they have been. The search for better government has led to visits to other countries and studies of how these other countries are trying to make government more effective. There has been an enormous international interchange and dialogue in recent years as ideas and approaches to better government have been explored (Weller & Davis 1996).

The public sector is not only in a politicised environment, it is also in one that changes in political complexion. And changes in political complexion cause changes in the public sector. From the 1970s onwards many electorates moved to the right and elected right-wing governments. These governments were critical of the public sector and were determined to act on what they saw as electoral mandates to shake up public sector organisations and even to privatise wherever they could. They put the public sector under a lot of pressure to increase efficiency.

Some 20 years on political demands for increased performance show no signs of abating. Measurement of performance to ensure strategic and performance goals are being met has been widely adopted. Moreover, in the UK, these goals are no longer seen as desirable only in efficiency terms. There are pressures on public sector organisations to base goals on public needs, including the needs of business and the voluntary sector as well as private citizens.

It seems unlikely in the next 5 or 10 years that this will change. Governments seem likely to continue placing the public sector under a critical and demanding political oversight. Public sector executives will be compelled to address performance goals. In the face of public dissatisfaction with poor services and high taxes, politicians will still be pointing to a gap between the outputs and outcomes of public sector organisations and the performance they require. They will continue to challenge the bureaucratic nature of the public sector and the limits of performance based on public resources.

This is not to argue that there is a simple continuity over the last decades. The changed political conditions in the 1990s brought to power politicians such as Clinton in the United States and Tony Blair in the United Kingdom. They were in favour of public services but not enamoured of bureaucratic styles of working. The previous decades had illustrated the price to be paid for bureaucratic ways of working. If changes are resisted over a long period of time, and if organisations lose sight of their duty to serve the public, then the public sector will be plunged into crisis and cutbacks. Politicians such as Clinton and Blair sought a 'Third Way' between bureaucratic systems and disintegration of the public services.

The Third Way politicians have identified the existence of cross-cutting issues which have risen up the public agenda—such as the environment, crime, social exclusion, drugs, etc.—and which are increasingly seen as requiring a response by a wide range of public sector bodies. For example, improving the health of the nation may be seen as dependent on job opportunities, levels of pay, housing, environmental standards, and many more things. Relying on a public health service to improve health standards all by itself is now seen as mistaken; it requires action on a broad front by many different public sector organisations. An integrated approach based on effective partnership working is seen as offering the best prospects of tackling cross-cutting issues. The importance of consulting the customer or public, and generally being responsive to the public, has also been a distinguishing feature of the Third Way agenda.

The recent rise of strategic management and its specific character within the public sector is a sign that public sector management has been placed under pressure by the political system to adopt a more proactive relationship to change. Elected politicians have most effect on top managers, especially the chief executives, who depend on the politicians for support. Consequently commitment to making the changes that are modernising the public sector is strongest in

the top ranks of public management. There is much less commitment among the lower ranks of managers and other employees.

Some managers believe that pressures on them are also increasingly coming from the public. They say the community is becoming
more demanding and less deferential. This may be the result of the
deepening hold of consumerist values within contemporary society.
Mellors (1996) has made this point about Australia, but similar
arguments appear in many countries. He predicts the public sector
will face continuing change from consumers:

> consumers are increasingly educated and demanding, both in respect of
> their consumption of private goods and services and, as consumers and
> funders, through taxes, of government services. This in turn is sharpening
> the focus of consumers/voters on quality as well as price, and generating
> more vigorous debate about the 'core functions' of government (Mellors
> 1996, p. 84).

It may be a side effect of the success of the private sector in offering
choice to the public and demonstrating an ability to develop very
rapidly many new products and services. Some top managers believe that the community expects more involvement in decision
making. Others want to boost involvement because they think
greater contact with members of the public will help them run
public services better. Some say they are being expected to enable
more involvement of the public by elected politicians. These are all
signs of the start of a shift in the relationship of public sector
organisations and the public. A much stronger ethos of serving the
community and putting the public first has begun to displace older
bureaucratic attitudes.

While political pressures, and to some extent public pressures,
have been the main factors bringing about strategic changes in the
public sector, it should be noted that there have been attempts from
within the public sector to bring about major change. In the 1980s
and early 1990s many public sector organisations joined the quality
movement and embraced ideas of continuous improvement.

STRATEGIC CHANGE

Chief executives and top management teams throughout the public
sector, now find themselves under enormous pressures to deliver the
changes the politicians are demanding. A new public sector is

emerging. The new public sector talks in terms of strategy rather than policy (Pettigrew et al. 1992). Major programme areas are strategy led rather than policy led. This is because the future of the public sector is being addressed in terms of a long-term agenda of strategic change to modernise public sector activities and services. The language (and thinking) of strategy fits this agenda for change, renewal, and innovation, better than the older language of policy and implementation. The language of strategy can better carry the long-term vision of modernisation than the bureaucratic language of policy making and implementation. Strategy is also a language that sits more comfortably alongside the entrepreneurial spirit being harnessed by the modernisation agenda than the conservative language of policy makers and implementers.

Public sector managers are learning how to use strategic management under these conditions of challenge and change. Management planning in the early years of public sector management reform produced a concentration on an annual planning cycle and led to short-term considerations of resource utilisation and contracting. The new public sector is more likely to be thinking 10 years ahead.

They are learning how to use strategy to reconstruct the public sector to align resources better with consumer interests, rather than provider interests. Strategic changes, therefore, imply the negotiation and adjustment of different interests and ideologies of the various stakeholders in the public sector. This makes the new public sector, as it modernises, a lively and challenging environment for the strategic manager.

CONTEXT

The point made above is that politicians have mainly mediated the public sector's relationship with the public over the last 50 years. In other words, the effects of environmental changes have impacted on the public services through the politicians. The current changes in the public sector have largely resulted from politicians' making changes to the legal and policy frameworks in which public services operate.

There is no turning the clock back to the public sector structures of the past. In the fields of health, education, local and central government the monolithic structures have been broken up and more fluid organisational structures created. Take the case of the

British civil service. In the decade following the late 1980s three out of every four civil servants were moved out of traditional departmental organisations and into discrete management units with strong performance management arrangements. This shift has been widely viewed as a success in terms of improved performance and cost savings.

In individual organisations there have been some trends towards decentralising responsibility for operational matters to service managers, leaving those in the organisational centre to take on a more strategic role. This has been happening in a range of public sector organisations. In essence, in Britain, this is the effect of setting up Next Steps agencies to handle the operational activities of government departments, leaving behind what was a policy function, but which is fast becoming a strategic function. We see the same decentralisation trends at work in local authorities, hospitals, and elsewhere (Pollitt et al. 1998).

The trend towards decentralisation has been under way for many years. A more recent development has been the pressure on the public sector to become more integrated. This has been expressed in Britain through the concept of co-ordinated action by partnership working. In late 1997, for example, Dobson, then the Secretary of State for Health, suggested that the strategies of organisations implementing government policy must be integrated to achieve success and that partnership was required.

These changes in legal and policy frameworks as well as changes in organisational frameworks provide the context in which public sector managers have been designing and trying out different ways of handling strategic changes.

APPROACHES TO HANDLING STRATEGIC CHANGES

In the past a combination of centralised decision making (policy making and budgetary processes) and strong professional cultures created bureaucratic organisations that found it difficult to communicate with the public and had difficulty in being responsive to the needs of service users. This was at its worst in professionally dominated organisations.

There were advantages to this older pattern of bureaucratic working. For instance, it left the professionals within public services much more discretion and autonomy in day-to-day decision making regarding service activities. There were advantages in this system for the elected politicians. While they had to submit themselves to the uncertainties of the electoral cycle every few years, in between time they were left with a free hand to style the organisation in line with their political objectives and priorities. The public was also able to leave conflict-prone and time-consuming decision making to the politicians, managers, and professionals. One of the biggest doubts about involving the public is indeed the question of whether the public has any interest in being involved. Will members of the public give up any of their free time to become involved in decision making?

For largely political reasons, the more bureaucratic styles of working are now generally criticised in the public sector. The earliest attempts to break with bureaucracy and introduce strategic change in the public sector made use of competition mechanisms and strengthened management hierarchies. In Britain the attempt to use an internal market to achieve greater efficiency had some important benefits in the National Health Service. The internal market succeeded in freeing up a lot of activities that had been stifled by the preceding bureaucracy. But there was a high price to pay. It emphasised the short term. It was expensive to administer. It fostered rivalry of a detrimental kind. The new policy thinking in a number of countries is now putting together a more complex mosaic of intervention. Competition and management are still important, but they are evolving in important ways.

The current approach encourages public sector managers to be pragmatic about using competitive mechanisms such as contracting out services. Where it is the best option, public sector managers should use open competition and contracts. Contracts and tendering are to be used wherever they offer improvements in the efficiency and quality of public sector activities.

This current approach manages change strategically. The new approach increasingly looks for strategic change to be handled through creative problem-solving approaches. It sits comfortably with the 1980s rejection of linear strategic planning, and the interest paid to more creative and intuitive forms of strategising. It also has a harder side. It encourages the use of strategic planning systems. These strategic planning systems have been, or are being, introduced in a number of countries as a result of decisions by governments.

It is concerned to involve the public and unleash the benefits of partnership working. The Third Way policy framework wants more open management. Being open is about being willing to inform and communicate. It is about a willingness to consult the public and other organisations. This openness is linked to responsiveness. The new policy thinking is about developing an openness and responsiveness to the public and partner organisations. This is intended to replace the secrecy and indifference of bureaucratic cultures, and the secrecy and competitive jockeying for advantage of contract cultures. The winners are intended to be the public, who should get better quality services as a result of increased openness and responsiveness. Many public sector organisations now make strenuous efforts to communicate with the public. They make better provision for enabling the public to gain information and access to services. These things are seen as important for modern, efficient, and effective public sector organisations.

Openness in management generally can lead to strategy formulation being carried out in a more open and inclusive way than in the private sector. Strategies for individual programme areas (health, education, etc.) are published and opened up to consultation and discussion. Of course, governments have long published consultation documents, but in the new public sector this consultation also concerns long-term strategy. Through the new consultation the public and partners are invited to contribute to the development of strategy thinking. The new public sector has recognised the variety of interests among stakeholders and pursues consensus, building a shared commitment to an agenda for change and modernising. In the process, the ideas and interests of the stakeholders are woven into the strategic vision. Strategy is, therefore, pluralistic in its creation and unitary in its aim.

How far a strategy-led public sector might further develop and displace bureaucratic decision making has, by definition, yet to be seen. However, we might note the way that long-term strategic planning and communications functions were being brought together in two British government departments in 1998. These were the Department for Education and Employment and the Department for Culture, Media, and Sport. In the light of the emphasis being put on public consultation and involvement and working with partners throughout the public sector, there is an obvious logic to this enrichment of the strategy function by a communications function. Alternatively, this could be just an indication that public relations thinking now dominates strategic planning!

There is a curious parallel between this development within government and developments in the US private sector. Heath (1997) has analysed the evolution of issues management as a form of strategic management in private businesses. He brings out how it draws on strategic planning and early public relations approaches. He defines its most contemporary form as providing strategic management with processes of two-way communication to reach constituencies in a way that is 'collaborative and long range rather than short term' (p. 16). This type of communications function is not just about issuing press releases and handling media relations to gain good publicity. If modern public sector management is serious about being open, involving the public, and working with partners, then two-way collaborative communications are critical for the formation and maintenance of strategies. Communications cannot be just a way of selling a strategic change decided on unilaterally by an organisation.

A key part of the new approach to strategic change is a move away from a 'tax and spend' philosophy to a more entrepreneurial view. This means taking a lot of trouble to identify public needs and then seeing how resources can be mobilised. This is consistent with the interest in research into public attitudes towards public services. In the new public sector there is a great interest in finding out what the public wants. There is a realisation that in the past the politicians and professionals made too many assumptions about what activities were of most benefit to the public. So the views of the public are being regularly sought to establish where improvements are needed. Surveys, complaint procedures, citizens 'juries', users' panels, neighbourhood and community forums are all being pressed into the service of greater responsiveness to the public. In the case of the British NHS, plans were announced in 1998 for an annual survey of 100 000 patients to help with assessing the quality of services.

The new public sector strives for integration of strategic changes. This can be seen at its clearest in the way in which legislation on federal agencies in the United States was implemented. The legislation—the Government Performance and Results Act of 1993 (GPRA)—has been seen as important in rebuilding public confidence in the efforts of government. It has not only instigated strategic planning across the board in US government agencies, it also requires individual agencies when preparing their strategic plans to consult with other interested parties. One of the early lessons of implementing this legislation was the need for further inter-agency co-ordination where there were overlapping responsibilities.

Such co-ordination is believed to be important if individual agencies are to achieve their strategic goals. Public sector executives must address public and social needs that cut across the mandates of a range of public sector organisations. So they must develop strategies which connect with, and complement, those of other public organisations. And, increasingly, there are demands for them to fashion strategic partnerships with organisations from other sectors.

Integration is not easy to achieve. In Britain, for more than 10 years, there have been repeated calls and demands for social services and health services organisations to work together. Progress has been variable. A 1998 report from the Social Services Inspectorate identified the need for improved working together on assessment, care planning, and discharge arrangements for elderly people. The aim of such partnerships is the provision of 'seamless' services to clients.

In the new public sector, organisations should not only be ensuring effective partnerships with other public sector organisations. The public sector now works with the private sector. In part this is the entrepreneurial approach to strategic change. It recognises the limited amount of public money available from taxation and the need to mobilise private resources for public purposes. This is encouraged by governments, and has produced a variety of schemes in different areas of public service. It has had the desired effect of adding private investment to that by government. The benefits have been seen in new hospital buildings, in schools, in waste management, and elsewhere.

REQUIREMENTS OF TOP MANAGEMENT

Many public sector managers over a long period of time feel they have been under pressure from politicians to absorb cuts in budgets. This can be seen as offering them a choice. Either the cuts have got to be passed on in fewer services or the quality of services has to be reduced. Consequently, some say they would like more honesty in the debate with the public about resources. They would like the public to know that a cut in budgets will mean fewer or poorer quality services. Of course, the implication of this is that they are absorbing cuts in budgets and are cutting services (extent or quality) without any communication of this fact to the public. This implies there is a low level of honesty in this relationship with the public. The providers of public services may feel that they have, for example, cut standards to spread their resources and cannot say publicly that they now provide a much less satisfactory service. In the case of English higher education, for example, university staff sometimes complain that there has been a massive expansion of student numbers without a commensurate increase in government funding. If there is a linear relationship between funding per student and the quality of education, which many professionals assume, then it may be supposed that standards have fallen correspondingly. (There is also another elitist argument that standards have fallen simply because more people have access to university and it is assumed that this must mean less able students who are generally allowed to pass by lowering standards.)

Perhaps there is an issue of honesty for those public sector top managers who blame the elected politicians for what they see as a deteriorating service when they themselves are not open to new ideas for how the public's needs can be met. There is an argument here about the responsibility of the public service not only to exercise probity in the use of public money but also to accept responsibility for ensuring that the activities and services of their organisations keep on evolving. To defend rigidity in these activities and services is to risk socially suboptimal levels of productivity. This all assumes that standards of productivity and quality are relative rather than absolute, and that, like the private sector, there should be a constant drive to raise standards and achieve continuous improvement.

There is a requirement that top managers deliver innovation as well as efficiency. While public sector managers at times see a simple correlation between budgetary inputs and the quality and extent of services, politicians, quite correctly, call for innovation and demand that managers do more with less. Innovation is a way of increasing the benefits to the public while reducing the financial costs. This is the essential idea of using innovation to increase consumer benefits and productivity. Private sector managers in a range of different industries have been forced by competition to introduce innovations in products and in business processes. It is not unknown for products such as computers, photocopiers, watches, cars, and so on to be increased in their functionality while prices are kept the same or even fall. Companies such as Toshiba, Canon, Swatch, and Ford have all shown that managers can respond to the innovation challenge that requires better and more reliable products to be produced with greater efficiency. There are many managers in the public sector who do indeed work hard to bring about innovations within the existing budgetary constraints, and who therefore show that innovation is one way of honestly maintaining the benefits to the public even in the face of budgetary pressures.

The elected politicians appear to be willing to share responsibility for innovation and change with public sector managers. This means that they no longer expect all changes in the public sector to be ordered from above by policy-making processes or to be legally mandated. They expect the managers to deliver much more accountable and responsive services. This is partly to be done through management tools such as strategic management, which institutionalises a new form of responsiveness to the public sector environment. This is a fundamental change in the value pattern of the public services.

Top managers have to provide the kind of leadership that sets ambitious goals for strategic changes and commands the respect and commitment of managers and employees. This may be why many of them do not deal with strategic change primarily through the use of authoritarian controls, but through strategic management processes. It has been apparent in mapping strategic management processes throughout the preceding chapters that strategic management in the public sector is less concerned with the analytical challenges of planning than it is with managing change in ways that secure political support and increase responsiveness to the public. It is also apparent that many of the processes—of preparing for strategic change, leading, changing, and building partnerships for change with the public and others—are aimed at addressing the rigidities of the organisation and its culture. Top managers, for example, have to build their leadership; they cannot take it for granted. They need to involve others in the organisation about thinking about the future. Once there is a strategic vision or intent and a strategic plan the top managers then have to pay attention to engaging employees with the process of implementation. They also have to use performance management and incentives to stabilise planned changes. Finally, in building relationships with the public, forming partnerships, and generally opening up the organisation they are often having to counter old-style professional attitudes, defensiveness, and even resistance. So in this specific character of strategic management in the public sector we see a reflection of the dilemma of top managers—how to enlist the rest of the organisation for the modernising of the public sector.

The credibility of the public sector is to a substantial extent in the hands of the top managers that head public sector organisations. This credibility has been severely questioned for over 20 years now, and its recovery rests upon their ability to develop organisations that deliver outcomes that meet public needs. The insecurity and pessimism which have pervaded the public sector since the welfare state began to falter in the 1970s will not be resolved by marginal strategic adjustments. It requires a major strategic transformation in the organisation and results of the public sector.

PLANNING AND PERFORMANCE MEASUREMENT REQUIREMENTS

Targeting strategic changes and then knowing if they are having their desired effects require public sector organisations to have a capacity for strategic planning and performance measurement. Hard work is needed to introduce and make strategic planning and performance measurement work effectively.

Making strategic planning work effectively means developing a greater capacity for targeting changes by better linking of public needs and resources. This probably requires two things above all else. First, there is a requirement to engage in open and honest dialogue with the public and partners about what needs there are and what resources the public and partners can contribute.

Second, and critical for the deployment of internal resources, there is a requirement to enlist the lower ranks of managers and other employees. There are many employees and professionals who do not like the disruptions and uncertainties created by continuous adjustments and the loss of autonomy implied by responsiveness to the public. If this turns into resistance then attempts to consult and engage with the public and partners will be harder. If new needs are identified through dialogue with the public and partners then the organisation may have to develop or redeploy the skills of managers and employees. It has to be faced here that serious efforts to improve the skills of individuals and the capabilities of the organisation to meet new public needs is often a long-term process taking at least three or four years if not more. This has implications for the time scales of planning and making strategic changes, and consequently for involving managers and employees.

If the commitment of managers and employees to making such changes work is patchy and implementation of change is poor, then dialogue with the public and partners will have been wasted and may end in frustration and disappointment. One way to deliver on this requirement is to involve lower ranks of managers and employees in strategic management processes. There may be support for strategic change by managers, professionals, and employees generally if they are offered participation in strategic management processes.

Developing a capacity for measuring performance may not sound very demanding. However, in the United States, the experience of initiating strategic planning in government agencies under GPRA 1993 in the mid 1990s suggested that there were some difficulties in setting strategic goals in results-oriented terms. It is natural that senior public sector executives might want to avoid setting strategic goals that would be a hostage to fortune. The UK experience with Next Steps agencies and key performance indicators shows that indicators can also change from year to year, making it difficult to track performance over time (Talbot 1996). The issue at stake in both cases is public accountability of those who are charged with leading and managing public sector organisations. This requires not only measurable goals, but also some stability in their expression to ensure comparability over time.

In many areas of the public sector it is not easy to compare performance over time. For example, have educational standards been falling or rising? If the health services have become more efficient, has it been at the cost of quality? Is the public sector now more streamlined and efficient—or is it simply doing less? In the case of UK local government there is evidence of a standstill over the short term. The Audit Commission has been publishing statistics on council performance since 1994. The publication of performance results appears to place the spotlight only on the best and worst performers, leaving the bulk of councils with an 'average' performance often unaffected. This is interesting in itself. It may show that the main forces at work in levering up performance are rivalry among the best, fear of getting special attention from government and shame among the worst. If the publication of performance statistics brought the councils' activities more to their publics' attention, would effects not have been seen across the board?

It is difficult to predict how strategic planning and performance measurement in the new public sector will fare in the next 10 years. The history of programme planning and budgeting (PPB) in the 1960s and 1970s shows that attempts to introduce modern management tools will encounter some resistance from older bureaucratic traditions of public service. Perhaps the acid test might be seen in how the new strategic plans relate to the powerful budgetary processes that are blamed by many for incrementalism in the public sector. If strategic planning is effectively introduced we might see budgeting following strategy rather than vice versa.

SERVING THE PUBLIC

Critically for the public services, politicians are expecting the public sector to ensure continuous improvements and increased responsiveness to the public. These are two of the central themes of the modernising agenda for the public sector.

For many years, some public sector managers may have hoped to deal with political pressures for change by conspicuous management initiatives aimed at developmental objectives while making only modest changes in services and activities (Wechsler & Backoff 1986). The developmental approach to dealing with political pressure involves management making highly visible moves, appearing keen and energetic, and using training and communication programmes to develop the organisation. False 'shows' of responding are recognised within public sector management. In the Bloomsbury DHA case briefly reviewed in Chapter 2, it was noted that management was expected to deliver a major process of retrenchment. The region had been in favour of merging two hospitals to achieve savings. Management in the DHA rejected this option but its own strategy for retrenchment had then failed. The evaluation of a regional officer was harsh: 'The idea of the merger was to force rationalization and I think that it has gone at a symbolic pace. They have done things to show that they were doing things, but it has only been at a pace that was conducive to keeping people off their backs' (Pettigrew et al. 1992, p. 92).

With the introduction of performance measurement and tougher audit and inspection regimes this option of making a false show of responding may be less viable in the future. Providing that performance is measured accurately and that targets and quality standards are credible and closely based on public needs, the public sector organisations will have to become better at complying with political pressures and public needs.

While this book has outlined the strategic change processes that are used to handle major strategic changes, there remains a question about how public sector organisations can upgrade their levels of effectiveness in order to deliver continuous improvement and responsiveness to the public. Many public sector organisations have strategic goals, performance management systems, partnership working, and consult and involve the public already. However, they may not be producing an adequate level of benefits to the public. Organisational processes and systems may not be adequate and may need improvement. What self-improvement goals should be set and in what order should they be tackled?

Attention to mechanisms for involving the public and partnership working deserve early attention because they promise to bring easy gains in performance as measured by the benefits to the public. They also create challenges to an organisation's activities that may create more readiness for change. Perhaps the second phase should concentrate on improvement objectives relating to management of the change process and the management of resources. The effectiveness of management in these two areas has critical implications for how much improved performance can be reaped from involving the public and partnership working. Finally, in terms of linking together operational activities and community needs, there is a need to improve strategic management processes. They form a mechanism that has the potential of integrating the involvement of the public, partnership working, and the effective management of change and resources. It is probably easier to refine and deepen strategic management processes when these other components are already in place and producing benefits for the public. It is also a mechanism

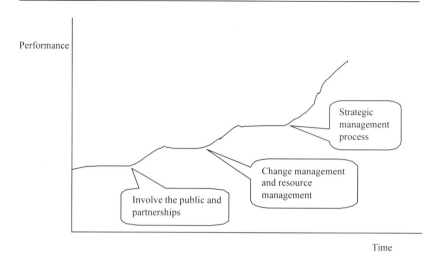

Figure 14.1   Organisational renewal programme: developing capacity for modernising

that can be used for community problem solving. As such, it enables evolving community needs to become the basis for strategic challenges to the organisation. This may sound like a huge burden for a management mechanism to bear, but Nutt & Backoff (1992) have argued that need volatility in society has created a turbulent environment for the public sector and that strategy development will need to be an ongoing activity. Figure 14.1 provides a graphic interpretation of these suggestions for a process of organisational renewal under the modernising agenda.

SUMMARY AND CONCLUSIONS

Strategic management faces a tough challenge in addressing the contemporary nature of the public sector. Few political leaders and managers in the public sector seriously think that 'carrying on as usual' or defending the status quo is acceptable.

Many politicians, in many different countries, are worried that they have lost the confidence of the public. They have often concluded that the loss of confidence may have something to do with public perceptions that politicians are failing to get value for money from public services and that taxes are already high enough.

There is a formidable list of requirements for strategic change in the public sector. In the light of this, simple models of strategy based on top-down strategic directives do not seem likely to be effective (Pettigrew et al. 1992). There are ideas about what is important and what works for public sector organisations. These ideas imply that successful top managers are skilled in preparing strategic changes, leading strategic changes, making and maintaining changes, and developing partnerships with the public and other organisations. These ideas are sufficiently coherent to be described as a model of public sector strategic change.

Modern public sector organisations are emerging that are good at involving the public and working with partners. These activities are, in effect, ways of building the external support that a public sector organisation requires to keep on operating. The whole status of public sector organisations has become more vulnerable, and there is an increasing need for communication and even dialogue with external constituencies to maintain public support. This is in part to establish the desirability of strategic and performance goals. It is in part to manage the issues that organised constituencies may raise and which if not handled properly will undermine confidence in the public sector organisation. Involving the public and working with partners also provide increased opportunities for relating a wider range of resources to public needs, thereby increasing and supplementing the organisational capacity of the public sector.

If the modernising of the public sector is not to be just hyperbole, more and more top managers will have to steer their organisations through major programmes of renewal. This is hard work. Staging or phasing self-improvement objectives over a period of time can be used to structure renewal programmes. A transition from bureaucratic organisations to strategy-led organisations that manage continuous improvement and responsiveness to the public will take some time to achieve.

Bibliography

Beckhard, R. & Harris, R.T. (1987). *Organizational Transitions*. Addison-Wesley, Reading, Mass.

Beedon, J. & Winchurch, D. (1995). Joining forces for strategic change, *People Management*, **1** (20), 42–4.

Berman, E.M. (1998). *Productivity in Public and Nonprofit Organizations*. Sage, London.

Bohret, C. (1993). The tools of public management. In Eliassen, K.A. & Kooiman, J. (eds), *Managing Public Organizations*, Sage, London.

Boyle, R. & McNamara T. (eds) (1996). *From Intent to Action*, Institute of Public Administration, Dublin.

Bryson, J.M. (1995). *Strategic Planning for Public and Nonprofit Organizations*, Jossey-Bass, San Francisco.

Bucher, R. & Stelling, J. (1977). Four characteristics of professional organizations. In R. Blankership (ed.), *Colleagues in Organization: the Social Construction of Professional Work*, Wiley, New York.

Bushnell, D.S. & Halus, M.B. (1992). TQM in the public sector: strategies for quality service. *National Productivity Review*, **11** (3), 355–70.

Corrigan, P. & Joyce, P. (1997). Reconstructing public management. *International Journal of Public Sector Management*, **10**, 417–32.

Crozier, M. (1964). *The Bureaucratic Phenomenon*, The University of Chicago Press, Chicago.

Eliassen, K.A. & Kooiman, J. (eds) (1993). *Managing Public Organizations*, Sage, London.

Flynn, N. & Strehl, F. (eds) (1996). *Public Sector Management in Europe*, Prentice-Hall Harvester Wheatsheaf, London.

Frost-Kumpf, L., Wechsler, B., Ishiyama, H.J. & Backoff, R.W. (1993). Strategic action and transformational change: the Ohio Department of Mental Health. In Bozeman, B. (ed.), *Public Management*. Jossey-Bass, San Francisco.

Gyford, J. (1991). *Citizens Consumers and Councils*, Macmillan, London.

Hamel, G. & Prahalad, C.K. (1994). *Competing for the Future*. Harvard Business School Press, Boston. Mass.

Heath, R.L. (1997). *Strategic Issues Management*, Sage, London.

Heymann, P.B. (1987). *The Politics of Public Management*, Yale University Press, London.

Holloway, J., Francis, G. & Hinton, M. (Public Interest and Non-profit Management Research Unit) (1999). *A Case Study of Benchmarking in the National*

Health Service, Open University Business School Working Paper Series, Milton Keynes.

Holzer, M. & Callahan, K. (1998). *Government at Work*, Sage, London.

Jorgensen, T.B. (1993a). Public resource allocation. In Eliassen, K.A. and Kooiman, J. (eds), *Managing Public Organizations: Lessons from Contemporary European Experience*, Sage, London.

Jorgensen, T.B. (1993b). Modes of governance and administrative change. In Kooiman, J. (ed.), *Modern Governance—New Government Society Interactions*, Sage, London.

Joyce, P. (1998). Management and innovation in the public services. *Strategic Change*, **7** (1), 19–30.

Kakabadse, A.K., Kakabadse, N.K. & Myers, A. (1996). Leadership and the public sector, *Public Administration and Development*, **16**, 377–96.

Kooiman, J. (ed.) (1993). *Modern Governance—New Government Society Interactions*, Sage, London.

Kooiman, J. and van Vliet, M. (1993). Governance and public management. In Eliassen, K.A. and Kooiman, J. (eds), *Managing Public Organizations*, Sage, London.

Leadbetter, C. & Goss, S. (1998). *Civic Entrepreneurship*, Demos, London.

Mellors, J. (1996). Managing and leading in the next century. *Australian Journal of Public Administration*, **55** (3), 83–9.

Meneguzzo, M. & Lega, F. (1999). From new public management to government modernisation: a comparative analysis of the role of innovation awards, paper presented at the Third International Research Symposium on Public Management, Aston University, Birmingham.

Nutt, P.C. & Backoff, R.W. (1992). *Strategic management of Public and Third Sector Organizations*, Jossey-Bass, San Francisco.

Osborne, D. & Gaebler, T. (1992). *Reinventing Government: How the Entreprenurial Spirit is Transforming the Public Sector*, Addison-Wesley, Reading, Mass.

Peters, T. & Waterman, R. (1982). *In Search of Excellence*, HarperCollins, New York.

Pettigrew, A., Ferlie, E. & McKee, L. (1992). *Shaping Strategic Change*, Sage, London.

Pollitt, C., Birchall, J. & Putman, K. (1998). *Decentralising Public Service Management*, London, Macmillan.

Porter, M. (1985). *Competitive Advantage*, Free Press, New York.

Social Services Inspectorate (1998). *'Getting Better?' Inspection of Hospital Discharge (Care Management) Arrangements for Older People*, Department of Health.

Talbot, C. (1996). Devolving from the centre: the UK experience. In Boyle, R. and McNamara, T. (eds), *From Intent to Action*, Institute of Public Administration, Dublin.

Weller, P. & Davis, G. (eds) (1996). *New Ideas, Better Government*. Allen & Unwin, St Leonards, New South Wales, Australia.

Wechsler, B. & Backoff, R.W. (1986). Policy making and administration in state agencies: strategic management approaches. *Public Administration Review*, **46**, 321–7.

Wilkinson, G. & Monkhouse, E. (1994). Strategic planning in public sector organizations, *Executive Development*, **7** (6), 16–19.

Wilkinson, D. & Pedler, M. (1996). Whole systems development in public services, *Journal of Management Development*, **15**, 38–53.

Index